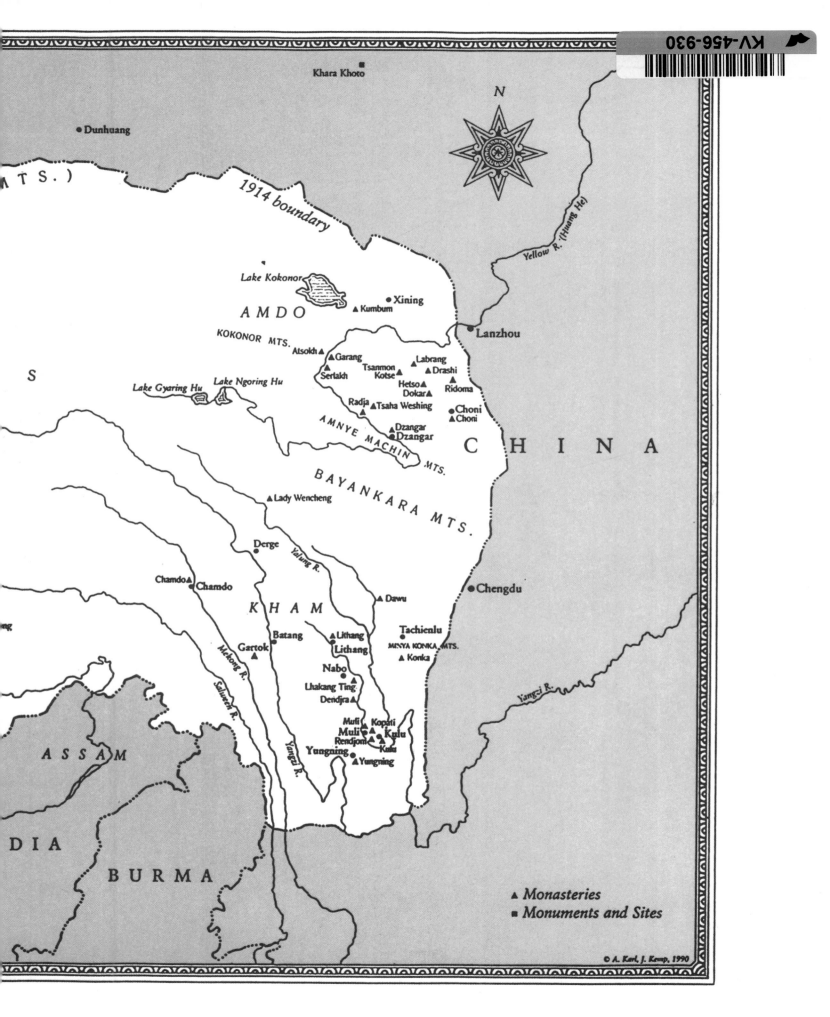

THE TIBETANS: LIFE IN EXILE

by Carol Barker

Mantra

in association with **The Tibet Foundation**

Dedication

For Lobsang and Yangchen Yeshi,
Nangsa Choedon, Dhola and Ngawang,
and all my Tibetan friends and
for all Tibetans, both in exile and in Tibet.

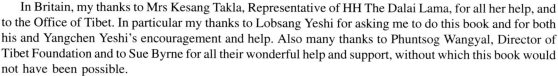

Acknowledgements

First of all I would like to thank His Holiness the Dalai Lama for granting me an audience and for His wonderful support and for making such a major contribution to the text of this book. Many thanks also to Tenzin Geyche Tethong for all his help and enthusiasm for this book.

In Britain, my thanks to Mrs Kesang Takla, Representative of HH The Dalai Lama, for all her help, and to the Office of Tibet. In particular my thanks to Lobsang Yeshi for asking me to do this book and for both his and Yangchen Yeshi's encouragement and help. Also many thanks to Phuntsog Wangyal, Director of Tibet Foundation and to Sue Byrne for all their wonderful help and support, without which this book would not have been possible.

In India, my thanks to Mrs Jetsun Pema, President of TCV Schools and her colleagues at TCV: Ven. Pema Dorje, Director of TCV, Tsewang Mingyur Khangsar, Principal of TCV, Ngawang Dorje, Director of Education, Mrs Tashi Lhamo, Sponsorship Co-ordinator and to Tashi Dolma and Tsering Dolma (Sponsorship Secretaries at TCV). My thanks also to people in the Education Office, in particular a big 'Thank you' to Nangsa Choedon for helping with my field research and her wonderful hospitality, especially on my arrival. My thanks to Kalon Tashi Wangdi, Minister for the Department of Information and International Relations and to Tempa Tsering (Secretary of the Department) and to people in his Department for all their help.

My particular thanks to Mr Yulgyal and to Mr Paljor at the Refugee Reception Centre, who helped me so much, both with the research for this book and in my relations with Tashi. My thanks also to Philippa and Jeremy Russell and to Jane Perkins for all their help and support. I would also like to thank Dhola, my interpreter. My special thanks to Ngawang, from Dolma Ling Nunnery and to Sonam and Tenzin Wangmo from TCV and thanks to my dear Tashi, for all your help and for contributing so much to this book.

Many thanks also to Ven. Saldon Kunga at Namgyal Monastery for his help and thanks to the monks at Namgyal Monastery for allowing me to photograph them. My very special thanks to Mr and Mrs (Dr) Jamling for all their kindness and hospitality during my stay at Tashi Choeling Monastery in Summer 1993. And thanks again to everyone for their continuing help and support during my second visit to Dharamsala from March to the end of May 1995.

Back in Britain, I would like to thank Phuntsog Wangyal and Tsering Dhundup for their help with the text, both with corrections and suggestions for improvement. Finally, my thanks to everyone else who has helped me to make this book, both in London and in Dharamsala.

Carol Barker
London , June 1998

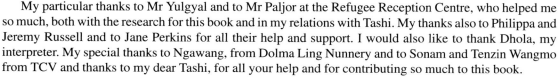

Published by
Mantra Publishing Ltd
5 Alexandra Grove, London N12 8NU

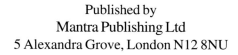

CONTENTS

Introduction 4

PART I: TIBET 'LAND OF SNOWS'
The Country and Its People 6
The Tibetan Empire and The 'Dharma' Kings 7
End of Empire and The Mongols 8
The British Connection & The 13th Dalai Lama 9
How the 14th Dalai Lama was Discovered 10
From Farmer's Son to Leader 11
The Tibetan National Uprising 12
Tibet under Chinese Occupation 13

PART II: EXILE IN INDIA
The Early Days 14
Making New Settlements 15
Newly Arrived Refugees 16
Tashi: His Escape Story 18
The Tibetan Children's Village (TCV) 20
Sonam: A Boarder at TCV 22
Tenzin Wangmo: A Day Pupil at TCV 24
Dharamsala: The Handicraft Centre 26
The Norbulingka Art Centre & The Master Thangka Painter 28
Namgyal Monastery: Saka Dawa & The Kalachakra Teachings 30
The Fire Puja Ritual (The Kalachakra Ceremony) 32
Gedhun Choekyi Nyima: the new Panchen Lama 34
The Tibet Support Workshop 36
Dolma Ling Nunnery and Ngawang's Story 38
Tashi: My 'Adopted' Son 40
Ling Rinpoche, the Reincarnation 42
H.H. the Dalai Lama: Leader of the Tibetans 44
A Private Audience with H.H. the Dalai Lama 46
Tibet Independence Day 47

FURTHER INFORMATION
Books for Further Reading 48
Tibet Foundation & List of Tibet Offices Worldwide 48

GLOSSARY 48
INDEX 49

INTRODUCTION

Tibet was invaded by China in 1950. Ten years later, after the Tibetan Uprising in March 1959, the Dalai Lama was forced to flee for his life and escape from Tibet over the Himalayan mountains to find refuge in India. Over the next three years, 85,000 Tibetan people followed their beloved leader, the Dalai Lama, over the dangerous high passes of the Himalayas, to escape persecution by the Chinese in Tibet.

Those early years of exile proved to be a desperate and difficult struggle for the Tibetan refugees. Many of them died of tuberculosis and malaria, diseases that they had never encountered before in the cold climate of Tibet. Today, there are 121,000 Tibetan refugees living in exile, mainly in India.

His Holiness Tenzin Gyatso, the fourteenth Dalai Lama, is the spiritual leader and the Head of State of the Tibetan people. His Holiness embodies the hope and inspiration for Tibetans living in exile. From the time that he first arrived in India in 1959, he has given Tibetan people the leadership and spiritual strength to overcome their terrible suffering and hardship of those early years in exile. He has helped them to rebuild their lives and their communities in India. It is now thirty-eight years since the Dalai Lama and the Tibetan refugees have been living in exile.

Since the Chinese invasion in 1950, the occupying forces have committed gross human rights violations against the Tibetan people, including murder, rape, torture, deportation and the destruction of family life. No Tibetan family has escaped from this tragedy. Over one million Tibetans have died at the hands of the Chinese since 1950.

Today many hundreds of Tibetans are imprisoned, beaten and tortured by the Chinese, usually for taking part in peaceful demonstrations for the independence of Tibet.

Between 1959 and 1961, the Chinese destroyed most of the six thousand monasteries in Tibet, reducing them to ruins. Their main aim was to destroy the basis of the Tibetan civilization and anything that gave Tibetans a distinct identity of their own.

Ever since the invasion, the Chinese have been

4

The British Connection and
The 13th Dalai Lama

The Manchu Emperor of China, Kang Hsi was able to take advantage of this state of affairs. He cleverly engineered a situation whereby he emerged as the liberator of Tibet, and installed the Seventh Dalai Lama in Lhasa in 1720. However, Tibetan independence was maintained (with Chinese troops protecting Tibet from Mongol and Ghurka invasions) but without the Chinese interfering in Tibet. From 1720 there were two men called Ambans (who were Representatives of the Chinese Emperor) living in Lhasa. But they had no power over Tibetan policy.

THE BRITISH CONNECTION

Towards the end of the 19th Century (during the time of the 'British Raj' in India) Britain signed several treaties with China over trade missions and border issues. They did not produce any meaningful results, until Britain signed a treaty with the Tibetans themselves.

At this time fears began to grow amongst the British Authorities, that Tibet might fall into the hands of the expanding power of Russia, with unfortunate consequences for British interests in India, and the Himalayan states. There were rumours of a secret treaty between Russia and Tibet that aggravated suspicions.

Finally, Britain felt that it had to act, and in 1904, the British despatched a military expedition under Colonel Francis Younghusband. They invaded Tibet, and reached Lhasa. The Tibetans could not hope to resist the more modern and powerful British guns and fighting force. In one engagement 600 Tibetans were mown down by Maxim guns. The 13th Dalai Lama fled to Mongolia, where he remained for four years.

The British persuaded the Tibetans into signing an Agreement on trade and border rights, an Anglo-Tibetan Convention. After establishing this Trade Agreement, the British left Tibet.

In 1910, when the Chinese army marched into Lhasa, the 13th Dalai Lama fled to India to find refuge under British protection. This was the first Chinese army that had ever been directed against the Tibetans, and this short period was the only time that China had tried to impose her authority by force. With the Chinese Revolution in 1911, whatever influence the Manchu Emperor in China thought that he had in Tibet, disappeared; the Chinese troops in Lhasa mutinied, and were sent back to China, via India and Hong Kong.

THE 13th DALAI LAMA THUPTEN GYATSO 1876-1933

He was a good diplomat and an astute politician, who understood the importance of establishing Tibet's position in the world. For this reason he issued a Proclamation of the Independence of Tibet in 1912. For the next twenty years the Dalai Lama governed Tibet, and it enjoyed complete peace, stability and independence. In 1913 there was a conference in Simla (India) between the British, Tibetans and Chinese, as equal partners, to agree on border issues, and to establish Political Statutes over Tibet. The Chinese never signed this, so Britain and Tibet concluded the Treaty. As long as China failed to acknowledge the Simla Convention, in the eyes of Britain, Tibet was de facto independent. The Treaty remained the practical basis on which a working relationship was maintained between Tibet and Britain, and later with independent India, until 1950.

Tibet remained neutral through both World Wars. During this time the 13th Dalai Lama experimented with modernisation. Officers in the Tibetan army were given training by the British; a hydro-electric plant was constructed in Lhasa, and the first motor-car rumbled across the High Plateau. The 13th Dalai Lama's death however in 1933, led to quarrels and intrigue.

(Below) The 13th Dalai Lama Thupten Gyatso 1876 -1933

How The 14th Dalai Lama was Discovered

EDUCATION OF A MONK

The Dalai Lama commenting on his education said, "The curriculum that I studied was the same as that for all monks pursuing a doctorate in Buddhist studies. It was very unbalanced and in many ways totally inappropriate for the leader of a country during the 20th Century. Altogether my curriculum embraced five major and five minor subjects. The former being Logic, Tibetan Art and Culture, Sanskrit, Medicine and Buddhist Philosophy."

(Below) The 14th Dalai Lama Tenzin Gyatso, aged 6, sitting on the Lion Throne in the Potala Palace (1940)

Following the death of the 13th Dalai Lama, Rating Rinpoche (a high lama) took over temporary control of the Government as the Regent. One of his first tasks was to find a new Dalai Lama. Tibetans believe that each Dalai Lama is a reincarnation of the previous Dalai Lama. It was the task of the Regent to find the young boy, who was the reincarnation of the previous Dalai Lama. But where should he look?

In 1935 the Regent visited the sacred Oracle Lake, Lhamo Lhatso, in the South-east of Lhasa. There, in the clear waters of the lake, he saw a vision. First he saw the Tibetan letters *Ah*, *Ka* and *Ma* float into view. These were followed by an image of a three-storied monastery with a turquoise and gold roof. Finally, he saw a small house with strangely shaped guttering. The Regent thought that maybe the letter Ah stood for Amdo Province.

In 1937 search parties were sent to all parts of Tibet. The search party that headed east to Amdo Province was led by Lama Kewtsang Rinpoche. When they reached Amdo, they found Kumbum monastery which had a turquoise and gold roof, as had been seen in the vision in the lake. And the letter *Ah* did seem to stand for Amdo, and *Ka* for Kumbum Monastery. Now they needed to find the small house. They began searching neighbouring villages. At last they saw a house with gnarled branches on the roof, and they thought that this might be where the child was.

The group of monks asked the people living there, if they could stay the night, without explaining the purpose of their visit. The leader of the search party, Kewtsang Rinpoche, disguised himself as a servant. The moment he entered the house, and sat down with the family, the youngest boy aged two, recognised him and called out 'Sera Lama, Sera Lama!'. (Sera was the name of Kewtsang Rinpoche's Monastery). Then the little boy climbed onto his lap, and asked to see his rosary, one which had belonged to the 13th Dalai Lama. Next day the monks left, only to return a few days later as a formal deputation.

This time they brought a whole variety of religious objects with them (drums, rosaries, and walking sticks) some of which had belonged to the 13th Dalai Lama, and some had not. The monks asked the little boy to choose some of the items. In every case, he selected only those things that had belonged to the 13th Dalai Lama saying, 'It's mine. It's mine!'. The monks also asked the child test questions, which he answered correctly. This, combined with the Regent's vision in the Oracle lake, of the letters *Ah* for Amdo, *Ka* for Kumbum, or *ka* and *ma* for Karma Rolpai Dorje's monastery above the village, convinced the search party that they had found the right child. The little boy, Lhamo Thondup, was later acknowledged to be the true incarnation of the Dalai Lama.

Word was sent back to Lhasa informing the Regent. But there were to be long delays. The local Governor of Amdo demanded a huge ransom to be paid to him, before he would allow the child to leave his Province. It took 18 months to raise the money. During this time the little Dalai Lama was taken to live in Kumbum Monastery with the monks, and his brother Lobsang Samten.

At last, in the Summer of 1939 they were allowed to leave. The little Dalai Lama travelled in a sort of palanquin carried by a pair of mules. He was accompanied by his parents, his brother, members of the search party, a number of pilgrims, some government officials, and a large number of scouts and muleteers. The caravan took three months of travelling over mountains, rivers and plateaux, in all weathers, to reach Lhasa in Central Tibet.

From Farmer's Son to Leader

During the journey, the Tibetan Government formally announced its acceptance of the child as the 14th Dalai Lama. He was brought into Lhasa in a magnificent procession, with people wearing brocade, costumes and jewellery, and holding silk banners and golden horns. It was a fantastic show of colour and pageantry with huge crowds of people and a special ceremony to welcome the child Dalai Lama back home. Then he was taken to the Norbulingka Palace to live.

On 22nd February 1940, the young Dalai Lama was taken to the Potala Palace, where he was officially enthroned as the 14th Dalai Lama, the Spiritual leader of Tibet. It was the first time that he had sat on the Lion throne, a vast jewel encrusted and beautifully carved structure. He was just four years old.

Soon after this, he was taken to the Jokhang temple, where he was inducted as a novice monk. This involved a ceremony known as the 'Ta-Phue' meaning 'cutting of hair'. From now on, he was to be shaven-headed and dressed in a maroon monk's robe. Then, in the final part of the ceremony, he gave up his name Lhamo Thondup, and was given the name Jamphel Ngawang Lobsang Yeshe Tenzin Gyatso.

As the Dalai Lama was too young to govern, effective power of government was held by the Regent, the Abbot of Rating Monastery. The young Dalai Lama lived at the top of the Potala Palace in winter, and at the Norbulingka Palace in summer.

From the age of six, the Dalai Lama was given strict religious training, and learnt to read and write. At the age of thirteen he was formally admitted to Sera and Drepung Monasteries to attend debates, and to practice dialectical discussion at large meetings.

With the end of the British Raj in 1947, India became independent. Two years later China, wanting to expand its Communist power and influence under the leadership of Mao Tse Tung invaded Tibet, and occupied the Eastern Provinces of Kham and Amdo.

The Tibetan Cabinet in Lhasa were dismayed. They made a special request that the Dalai Lama, now aged fifteen, should assume control of the State from the Regent, three years earlier than the usual age of eighteen. The ceremony took place on 17th November 1950 and Tenzin Gyatso, the 14th Dalai Lama, found himself the undisputed leader of six million Tibetan people, facing the threat of a full-scale war with China.

His first task was to appoint two new Prime Ministers, one layman and one monk. The Dalai Lama also had to continue his studies of Buddhist Scriptures and philosophy. It was not until much later, in 1959, that he had to take his final examinations. He passed

with honours and was awarded the highest Geshe Lharampa Degree (Doctorate of Buddhist Philosophy).

The Dalai Lama also had to attend to the affairs of State. In 1954, he went to Peking for peace talks with Mao Tse Tung and other Chinese leaders.

THE CHINESE INVASION OF TIBET

In 1950, the People's Liberation Army entered Tibet, and defeated the Tibetan army at Chamdo. At this point, Tibet appealed to the United Nations: Britain and India moved that the subject should be deferred, and it was adjourned. As a result Tibet was obliged to take part in talks in Peking which led to the notorious 'Seventeen Point Agreement' for the 'peaceful liberation of Tibet' in 1951. The conditions under which the Treaty was signed were shameful. The Tibetan delegates were given a blunt choice - to sign the document, or face war! They were even prevented from seeking the Dalai Lama's advice; and the Chinese had forged copies made of the official seals of the Dalai Lama, so that the Agreement could be stamped, without the knowledge of the Dalai Lama.

In 1956 the Dalai Lama travelled to India, where he met Prime Minister Nehru and Chou En Lai, the Chinese Foreign Minister. He tried to obtain recognition for Tibet's independence from China, and help to end the Chinese occupation. However, help was not forthcoming. Nehru just assured him that Tibetan Autonomy (the right to govern one's own country) would be respected, and 'Reforms' would not be forced on Tibet by the Chinese.

17-POINT 'AGREEMENT'

Soon after he was made the political leader of Tibet in 1950, the Dalai Lama decided, in the face of an advancing Chinese army, to move secretly to Dromo in Southern Tibet. There, he took refuge in a monastery. The Dalai Lama recalls: "At the monastery, I had an old Bush radio receiver. Every evening I would listen to the Tibetan language broadcasts of Radio Peking...A harsh crackling voice announced that a 17-Point 'Agreement' for the Peaceful Liberation of Tibet had been signed by representatives of the Government of the People's Republic of China and what they called the 'Local Government of Tibet'. Clause 1 stated that 'The Tibetan people shall unite and drive out imperialist aggressive forces from Tibet. The Tibetan people shall return to the big family of the Motherland - the People's Republic of China.' What could it mean... The idea of Tibet 'returning to the Motherland' was a shameless invention. Tibet had never been part of China."

(Above) The Dalai Lama (left of centre) with the Panchen Lama, on their arrival at Peking for the peace talks in 1954. He is flanked by Chou En Lai (far right).

The Tibetan National Uprising

A TIBETAN GENOCIDE

Following the events of 1959 in Tibet, two reports were issued by the International Commission of Jurists which first raised the charge of genocide and specified that human rights had been violated in sixteen ways, including murder, rape, torture, destruction of family life and deportation. These atrocites and sufferings fill the accounts of refugees and no Tibetan family is free of the memory of this tragedy. The Dalai Lama stated that between 1955 and 1959, 65,000 Tibetans were killed and at least 10,000 children deported. The Chinese- controlled Radio Llasa announced on 1st October 1960 that in the first year following the 1959 Uprising. 87,000 Tibetans were killed in Central Tibet alone. A pooled eye-witness report confirms that within a period of 17 days in 1966, 65,000 Tibetans were executed in and around Lhasa.

Over 1 million Tibetans have now been killed by the Chinese.

(Below) Members of the Tibetan Resistance Force in Lloka (Southern Tibet) in 1959

The 'Democratic Reforms' (as the Chinese called them) had in fact already been started in some parts of Kham and Amdo, the east of Tibet, as early as 1952-53. The Chinese tried to artificially create, and impose, a 'Class Struggle' on the Tibetan society. More roads were built, with the aid of large numbers of Chinese workers. In order to feed them the Chinese started to 'borrow' and then to buy stocks of food, causing severe inflation. Taxes were imposed, properties were confiscated and executions of Tibetan people followed.

THE NATIONAL UPRISING

The Tibetan guerilla movement started in East Tibet in 1953. It soon became widespread. Vast numbers of Chinese settlers started to be brought into the Chamdo area, and the Chinese made the fatal move of trying to disarm the Khampa people.

By 1954 a number of atrocities had been committed by the Chinese. Tibetans who resisted them were rounded up. They were called 'Reactionaries' and 'Serf-owners' and executed by the Chinese. In the small town of Doi in Amdo, in 1953, before a horrified crowd, 300 out of 500 people were shot in the back of the head. The Chinese threatened the rest of the population with the same fate if they opposed the Chinese regime.

In August and September 1954, the *New York Times* and the *Guardian* reported that 40,000 'farmers' had taken part in an uprising in south-east Tibet.

Meanwhile, as early as 1952, the 'People's Movement' Mimang Tsongdu, an underground organization, and the first Tibetan National Party appeared. They organized Tibetans into huge demonstrations of protest against the Chinese. Poster campaigns were carried out, demanding that the Chinese leave Tibet. The leaders were imprisoned.

Since 1952 the Chinese had been forcibly taking young Tibetan children from their parents, and sending them to China to Beijing and Chengdu to study at the Minorities National Institutes. More than 30,000 children were sent to China between 1952 and 1969. They were given a rigorous programme of indoctrination in communism, and the Chinese version of Tibetan history.

In Kham, in eastern Tibet, the 'Kanting Rebellion' of 1955-56 started, with the Tibetans launching a major guerilla offensive against the Chinese. This spread to Amdo Province in 1958, with the fiercest fighting around Lithang, Bathang, Chamdo and Kanze. A full-scale war was being waged, which the world never know anything about at all. The Chinese reprisals were terrible. Their aeroplanes and modern military weapons bombed Lithang monastery flat. Villages and Tibetan encampments were bombed and machine-gunned from the air. Thousands of Tibetans were killed. Almost a whole generation of Tibetans were killed.

It was at this time that the American CIA began to take an interest in what was happening in Tibet. It is one more tragic irony of the Tibetan struggle, that although the Tibetans appealed to the whole world for help, it only came from the Americans and was given simply to exploit the Tibetans as an anti-Communist force. Aid from the CIA was at its height during 1964-74 and enabled Tibetan guerilla fighters to operate from Mustang in Nepal. Much was made of exposing this 'CIA connection' at a time when it was fashionable to attack American foreign policy. However, the CIA had absolutely no effect on the final course of events.

By 1958, 15,000 families from the Kham region had become refugees. They drifted into Lhasa and then moved south to Lhoka. It was in South Tibet that the famous 'Four Rivers and Six Ranges' Resistance group was formed, under the leadership of Gonpo Tashi Andru-tsang. By now, fighters from all over Tibet had joined the Khampa movement. One of their slogans was: WE WOULD RATHER LIVE FOR ONE DAY AND DIE UNDER THE BUDDHA, THAN LIVE FOR A HUNDRED YEARS...UNDER ATHEIST RULE. Leaders of Mimang Tsongdu and the Khampas, saw force as the only solution. However, the Dalai Lama and the monastic community condemned the use of force, whilst the Tibetan Government dithered, holding out hopes of appeasement.

The Dalai Lama's Escape : Tibet Under Chinese Occupation

It was in this highly charged atmosphere, in early March 1959, that the Dalai Lama, then aged twenty-four, was invited to a Cultural Performance by the Chinese People's Liberation Army, but asked to come without his usual bodyguards.

This sparked off a mass spontaneous uprising in the capital on March 10th. Thousands of Tibetan refugees, who had flooded into Lhasa, mounted a demonstration against the Chinese. They feared that the Dalai Lama would be kidnapped and smuggled to Peking (now Beijing) or even worse, that he would be imprisoned and executed.

So 30,000 men, women and children made their way to the Norbulingka Palace, to watch over their precious Dalai Lama. It became obvious that the Chinese were soon going to attack the Norbulingka Palace. So the Dalai Lama, along with his family, decided to escape on March 17th 1959.

THE DALAI LAMA'S ESCAPE

This had to be carried out with total secrecy. The Dalai Lama disguised himself as a common Tibetan soldier. At 10pm on 17 March, 1959, he left the Norbulingka Palace. An hour before his mother, elder sister, youngest brother and maid had all left, in similar disguise. In his own 'patrol', was the Lord Chamberlain, the Chief Abbot, and the Commander of the body guard, his brother-in-law.

The story has a miraculous quality, because that very night there was a huge sandstorm, which dimmed the Chinese searchlights scanning the countryside, and helped to protect the Dalai Lama and his people, to make their escape to the Himalayas.

After several days of walking and riding over the perilous high mountain passes and battling through snow storms, ice and rain, they reached India, and safety on the other side. It was one of the most dangerous and dramatic escape stories of this century.

THE CHINESE ATTACK LHASA

It was a few days after the Dalai Lama had left, that the Chinese generals realised that their prized possession had fled the palace. On 20th March 1959, the Chinese shelled the Potala Palace in Lhasa. The next day the *Times* carried the headline: "FIGHTING IN LHASA. REVOLT AGAINST THE CHINESE." The Chinese bombed the Norbulingka Palace and the huge crowds of Tibetans who had gathered to protect their Dalai Lama.

An estimated 40,000 Tibetan people were killed by the Chinese during that time in Lhasa. Their bodies were heaped into mass graves or burned.

The Chinese at once abandoned their 'gradual' approach to 'Liberation', and dissolved the Tibetan Government. Reprisals and executions were carried out. They dissolved the monasteries at the outset, forcing out the hundreds of monks.

The Chinese then rounded up members of the Tibetan aristocracy who were landowners, government officials in positions of authority, high lamas and leading monks and scholars. They were subjected to torture and beatings and many died in 'Thamzing Class Struggle' sessions; others were imprisoned, sent to prison labour camps to work as slave-labour and died from torture and starvation. Between 1959 and 1961 the Chinese destroyed most of the 6,000 Monasteries in Tibet, reducing them all to ruins. The main aim was to destroy the basis of Tibetan civilisation or anything that gave Tibetans a distinct identity of their own. Over one million Tibetans have died at the hands of the Chinese since 1950. It was Genocide.

(Above) The ruins of monasteries destroyed by the Chinese. There were over 6000 monasteries in Tibet before 1959. The Chinese destroyed most of them between 1959 and 1961. Today, only part of thirteen monasteries remain. This photograph shows some of the rebuilt temples of Ganden Monastery. Rebuilding of some of the temples took place in the 1980's.

(Below) The Dalai Lama's escape from Tibet. He is near the front, riding a white pony, disguised as an ordinary Tibetan soldier. It was a hazardous journey, riding and walking through blizzards over dangerous mountain passes, camping in tents and battling against exhaustion and illness, before reaching the safety of India.

PART 2 : Exile in India
The Early Days

THE TIBETAN PARLIAMENT

Since 1963, there have been important changes to the Tibetan Parliament. In 1991, the Charter for Tibetans in Exile was adopted by the Assembly of Tibetan People's Deputies, who are the elected representatives of the Tibetans and are known as the Tibetan Parliament in Exile. Under the Charter, the Council of Ministers of the Tibetan Government are elected by the Parliament and no longer appointed by the Dalai Lama. The Government is therefore responsible to the Parliament and the Parliament is responsible to the people.

(Above) The Dalai Lama with Prime Minister Nehru in April 1959

The first sight that people in India had of the Dalai Lama was of him emerging from the mountain mists like a vision, surrounded by his people, descending from the snows of the Himalayan mountains.

Both he, and the Tibetans who had fled with him, had left everything behind, their homes, their possessions, and their country. Now they were refugees in a foreign land.

They were met by Indian border guards and some Indian officials, who escorted them to the town of Bomdila. After a few days rest, the Dalai Lama travelled by train to Mussoorie, a small town in the Himalayan foothills. On the train journey he was greeted by crowds of Indians shouting: "LONG LIVE THE DALAI LAMA!" The Indian people gave their guest a tumultuous welcome.

Meanwhile thousands of Tibetans began fleeing from persecution in Tibet. They had to take the most dangerous routes, climbing up to heights of 16,000 feet and more, to avoid being killed by Chinese soldiers, and bomber planes. Many of the Tibetans died on the journey. Most of these were babies, children and the elderly. By 1965 there were 85,000 Tibetan refugees who had fled into exile in India.

The Tibetan refugees arrived in India in the remote north eastern States. It was here that the Indian Government set up temporary camps. In the hot and steamy jungle of Assam, a transit camp called Missamari, was set up for about 12,000 refugees, living in 300 flimsy bamboo huts. And further west in Bengal, was a former prisoner of war camp at Buxa Duar.

Tibetans lived there in thirty concrete barracks surrounded by barbed-wire fences. Overstrained Indian officials, doctors and nurses battled against epidemics of cholera, dysentery, malaria and tuberculosis that raged through the camps. Many Tibetans died of these diseases.

Out of the many thousands of monks that were in Tibet in 1959, only 1,500 lamas and monks managed to escape to India in those early years. They were separated from their countrymen, and reassembled at Buxa Duar camp. It was decided, that if religious scholarship and practice were to be preserved, then the lamas and monks must be given a supportive environment. The situation today, proves that the decision was wise. From this nucleus of 1,500 lamas and monks (some of whom stayed at Buxa Duar for the entire eleven years of the camp's existence) came many of the scholars who have rebuilt Tibet's monastic tradition in exile.

Most of the people who followed the Dalai Lama into India in 1959 were peasant farmers and yak herdsmen and their families. Most of the Tibetan upper classes, including aristocrats, landowners, high lamas and monks, and Tibetans in positions of authority, died at the hands of the Chinese.

The peasant farmers and nomads who did manage to escape to India in 1959, were illiterate. While they were still living in temporary refugee camps, the Indian Government employed them to build the Himalayan mountain border roads, paying young and old men and women a few rupees a day. It was gruellingly hard work. Not only this, but diseases like TB and malaria were sweeping through the refugee camps where they were living, and many more people died.

The Dalai Lama was faced, at the age of 24, with a new and desperate challenge, to turn the tragedy of being a homeless refugee into a period of positive activity and to bolster the hopes and spirits of his people.

In 1961 Prime Minister, Jawaharlal Nehru, personally selected Dharamsala to be the permanent home for the Dalai Lama. From there he was able to start building a new base for the Tibetans in exile in India.

It was in 1963, that the Dalai Lama first drew up a Draft Constitution for Tibet, in which is embodied a democratic form of Government. This formed the basis for the Government-in-Exile to work on, with elected representatives taking the major role in the Government.

Making New Settlements

Today, it is the 'Kashag', the Council of Ministers, and the Tibetan Parliament (a democratically elected body) who administer the affairs of the Tibetan people in exile. The Tibetan Government administers through a number of departments - Home Affairs, Education, Health, Religion and Culture, and International Affairs.

One of the first tasks of the Dalai Lama and his newly formed Government, was to find a solution to the vicious circle of poverty, rootlessness and danger faced by the Tibetan refugees working on the roads. They needed a more settled life, and a better way of earning a living. In consultation with the Indian Government a solution was found. The answer lay in farming. But there was no land available in Northern India. So a plea went out to State Governments in the south.

The Karnataka, and other State Governments, came up with offers of land, but they were densely forested areas. However, following the Indian Government's approval, the first batch of Tibetan refugees set out in December 1960, to the 'unknown land' in Karnataka, way down in the South of India. It was terribly hard for those early refugees; many died from sheer anguish and despair, while tropical diseases took their toll. But in the end, they won through. The Tibetans were able to fell the virgin forest, to build their own houses, to cultivate the land with new crops, and to support themselves.

Today, thirty-eight years later, the Tibetan refugee farming communities cover 11,964 acres of cultivated land, which support around 30,000 refugees. The most successful crops, after twenty experimental years, are maize and millet. A family of five people usually owns four acres of land. They can grow just enough food crops to sustain themselves at subsistence level. Most households keep a cow or two, and sell any surplus milk to co-operatives.

The two settlements, Bylakuppe and Mundgod, in the south of India, are today the largest and most self-contained of the fifty-seven Tibetan communities scattered throughout India.

It is here also, in the heart of the biggest Tibetan community in the south of India, that the three main Gelugpa monasteries - Sera, Drepung and Ganden - have been re-established, along with Kagyu, Sakya and Nyingma monasteries. These Monastic Universities from Tibet have risen once more in modest buildings amidst the maize and millet fields in Karnataka State. They provide the main training ground for the young Tibetan monks living in exile.

Today, there are 121,000 Tibetan refugees living in exile, with the majority of them in India. They are living in settlements on land that was provided by the Indian Government. There are settlements also in Nepal, Sikkim and Bhutan.

Outside India, there are Tibetans living in exile in Switzerland, Canada, the United States, Britain, France, Germany, Sweden, Holland and other countries. However, for Tibetan refugees living in exile in whichever country, the centre and heart of the Tibetan community is where the Dalai Lama lives, and that is in Dharamsala.

I travelled to Dharamsala in Northern India and lived there for five months, to find out for myself what life was like for Tibetans living in exile. I also met the newly arrived Tibetan refugees. Thirty-eight years after China's invasion of Tibet, refugees still continue to make the dangerous journey across the Himalayan mountains to escape persecution by the Chinese occupying forces.

(Below) Newly arrived Tibetan refugees at Missamari Camp in Northern India, May 1959

Newly Arrived Refugees

DIPLOMATS VISIT TIBET

From the 16th-22nd May 1993 an EC delegation of ambassadors and senior diplomats visited Lhasa on a human rights fact-finding mission. There was a large demonstration by Tibetans against the Chinese occupation of Tibet. At least a hundred Tibetans were arrested and imprisoned.

Letters from local Tibetans addressed to the United Nations, the EC ambassadors and the World Human Rights Organisations were handed over to the ambassadors. The letters gave an account of how the Chinese were destroying the Tibetan culture and identity under the guise of pursuing a policy of political and economic openness.

(Below) Newly arrived refugee children at the Reception Centre in McLeod Ganj, awaiting their turn to be sent to one of the TCV schools in Northern India.

When the Tibetan refugees first arrive in Dharamsala, they go to the Reception Centre in Mcleod Ganj. I went there to see Mr Yulgyal, and he talked to me about the refugees and the Centre.

"It was in 1969 that the Chinese closed the borders. Tibet was completely cut off from the outside world for ten years. Then in 1979 the Chinese began to relax the regulations at the borders between Tibet, Nepal and India, and to allow some Tibetans to have permits to come over to visit their relatives in India and then to return to Tibet.

"From 1979 onwards, Tibetans began to escape as refugees to India. At first there were only a few people coming over. But gradually more and more refugees came. In 1989, 689 Tibetan refugees fled from Tibet. Then in 1990, all of a sudden, the numbers of refugees coming over increased to 2,066. That was when this Office was started at the Reception Centre in Gangchen Kyishong. But at that time we did not have a hostel, or anywhere for the refugees to stay. So in March 1991 we built dormitories and offices here in Mcleod Ganj. In that year there were 2,725 refugees who had escaped from Tibet to India. By 1992 this had increased to 3,374.

So there has been a steady increase of refugees every year.

"Most of the people come from the Eastern part of Tibet, formerly Amdo and Kham. The most dangerous part of their journey is when they have to walk over the high mountain passes of the Himalayas following the escape routes. Then, as they reach the border between Tibet and Nepal, the Nepalese Border Police harass them. The Border Police are paid by the Chinese to send back escaping refugees to Tibet. So, unless the Tibetan refugees can pay huge bribes to the Border Police, they are handed back to the Chinese authorities in Tibet, or even shot. There have been many cases when Tibetan refugees have been shot dead when they were travelling through Nepal.

"The refugees are not really safe until they reach our Reception Centre at Kathmandu. After two or three days, they travel on a special bus to our Reception Centre in Delhi.

"Most of the refugees, who are monks and nuns, are sent directly from Delhi to Tibetan monasteries in South India. The other refugees stay in Delhi and then continue their journey by bus to Dharamsala. As soon as they arrive they go straight to the Reception Centre, where we provide them with free food and accommodation. Within a day or two, the new arrivals have to go to Delek Hospital for a general health check. If any of them have tuberculosis they are kept in the TB Sanatorium.

"The majority of people escaping from Tibet today are monks. They were persecuted by the Chinese in Tibet, and were not allowed to practise their Religion. So they come to India to be able to continue their religious life. We help them to join the right monastery, according to the sect they belong to.

"The second largest group of refugees are farmers and nomads, mostly job-seekers. I should explain that there is no scope or possibility for Tibetans aged from 18-30 to get jobs in Tibet. All the jobs are reserved for the Chinese. There is such a vast 'Population Transfer' with thousands of Chinese people moving into Tibet, that it is virtually impossible for Tibetans to get jobs in the towns and cities in Tibet. The only work that they might find are labouring jobs in remote areas in the countryside.

"So most of those Tibetan refugees, who are above the age of 28, are job-seekers. We ask them to find their own jobs here. But we give them six months

support, as well as providing them with bedding and other essentials. So we are taking good care of them.

"The third group of refugees coming over here are children who are escaping in order to get a good education. In Tibet, education does not go beyond primary school level. Earlier, parents or close relatives used to come over with the children. But six or seven months ago, parents started sending their children over to India with a guide, or a group of people. This has meant that the Tibetan Children's Village (TCV) in Upper Dharamsala is overflowing with children. So now the newly arrived refugee children are sent to a new TCV School in Bir Village.

"When the refugee children first arrive, we try to sort them out according to their age groups. The children below thirteen are mostly sent to the TCV. There is also another home in Mussoorie run by the Tibetan Homes Foundation. We have to arrange for a quota of children to be sent alternately to these two Homes. Then there are the children aged fourteen to seventeen. We send them to Bir Open School, which is under the TCV Administration.

"Many of the young people aged eighteen to twenty-six are illiterate. But they are really keen to learn. So for them, we have created a Transit School. We give them non-formal education there. Then they can either go on to the Open School to continue their studies, or do a vocational training in carpet weaving or carpentry. We do everything we can to provide for them. But with more refugees coming over, the situation is becoming increasingly difficult."

In 1993, 3,766 refugees arrived in Dharamsala. However, by 1994, there was a change, both in the circumstances, and in the policy of the Tibetan Government, towards the refugees arriving from Tibet. Genuine refugees fleeing from persecution, such as monks and nuns or children seeking education, continued to be welcomed and looked after. But people aged over eighteen, who were job-seekers, were to be disappointed. There are no more jobs available for them in India.

Mr Yulgyal explained, "The policy of the Tibetan Government in Exile, as well as the Reception Centre, is that those Tibetans who are now living in Tibet should be encouraged to remain there, as the transfer of the Chinese population is going on in such enormous numbers. At the end of 1994 we revised our Education Programme at the Transit School for these students

aged over eighteen, to one year. During the year, they will have a crash course in the Tibetan and English languages, and they will have a lot of talks on Tibetan culture and identity. We want them to return to Tibet, and to spread the word amongst the Tibetan people living in the rural areas, and to explain how the Tibetan communities have been established, and how the Democratic Exiled Government has been formed in India. These things will really encourage the Tibetans living in Tibet. That is our main objective."

(Below) Some monks and nuns who have just arrived, July 1993

DIPLOMATS VISIT TIBET

The *Tribune* reported: "Between 1000 and 3000 Chinese pour into Tibet every day. In areas such as Kongpo in Southern Tibet, there are about twenty-five Chinese to every single Tibetan. At the same time the Chinese authorities force women to undergo abortions and sterilisations...Without identity papers or ration cards, Tibetans are denied the right to schooling and work and are deprived of their citizenship."

(Above) Job-seekers with two monks in the Reception Centre

Tashi: His Escape Story

Dangers of Escape

"The Nepalese police at the border of Tibet and Nepal are paid by the Chinese to hand over escaping Tibetan refugees," Mr Paljor told me. "The Tibetan refugees have to then offer even more money than the Chinese otherwise they are handed back to the Chinese. In 1991 there were two Tibetan brothers. They were among a group of seven Tibetans on their way to Katmandu. After they had crossed the border to Solokhumbo, the Nepalese police arrested them and demanded money. As they didn't have any money, a row broke out. The older brother tried to escape and run away and the police opened fire and shot him dead at point blank range."

(Above) Tashi, a newly arrived refugee, now safe at the Reception Centre in Dharamsala, after his harrowing escape from Tibet.

Twelve year old Tashi was one of the refugee children who had arrived recently from Tibet. He had suffered from severe frostbite on his feet, during his escape to India and had been receiving treatment at the Delek Hospital in Dharamsala. He was now well enough to stay at the Refugee Reception Centre, which is where I met him.

Tashi was born and brought up in Shigatse, where he lived with his parents, his younger sister, and his aunt and uncle. He went to a primary school until he reached Class 5 at the age of eleven. But that was as far as he could go. As a Tibetan child living under the Chinese occupation, there was no chance of Tashi getting a secondary education.

Tashi's parents were very worried about his future. Then they heard from a neighbour that there were good schools in India for Tibetan children. So they decided it would be better to send him there, so that he could get a good education.

Tashi told me about his escape and how he had risked his life walking over the high Himalayan mountains.

"My parents asked some people to bring me here to India. There was a business man, a trader from Kanze, who often went from Shigatse to the Nepal border.

"He helps Tibetan refugees to escape by taking them to the border for a fee. I joined the group in Shigatse. There were seven children, two girls and five boys, all younger than me. The youngest was a boy who was only eight years old. The other people escaping were adults. There were thirty-two of us altogether travelling from Shigatse to India.

"My parents and the others, paid money to the businessman, and he hired a truck and driver. We boarded the truck in Shigatse and were driven as far as Tingri. From Tingri we started walking for about eighteen hours to Rongshar, which is on the Tibetan side of the border with Nepal. We had to take the escape route, as we did not have permits. We walked around Rongshar, avoiding the town, the police patrols and the border guards, who might have caught us and sent us back.

"It was already snowing, so we had to walk through the snow. This was March and it was bitterly cold. We carried on walking for about ten more days through thick snow, over more than ten snow-capped mountains, to reach Solokhumbo near Namchi in Nepal.

"Some nights we spent in caves, and others, in friendly villages. We were carrying some food with us, mainly tsampa, which is made of barley, water and butter. For water we melted the snow.

"We were divided into groups of seven people. Each group had a kettle. We cut branches from the trees, and made a wood fire to melt the snow in the kettle, for our drinking water. While I was walking in the snow my feet were frozen. Then on the way the weather improved and there was sunshine. We came to a village where there were some houses. The villagers warned me not to go near the fire. As I was so cold, I didn't take any notice, and I went and sat close to the fire. Then my toes started swelling up. They were very painful. But as my friends were already leaving, I had to join the group. I kept walking. Then, on the part of my toes which were swollen, sores appeared. Pus came out of these sores. It was frostbite. The pain in my feet was terrible. But I had to carry on with the journey. I wanted to die, I felt that I just could not go on. The guide kept saying: Come on! Keep going! We'll reach the border soon. It's just around the corner. But of course it wasn't. I kept thinking that India must be such a beautiful place and that it was full of golden temples. The pain in my toes and feet was terrible. But I had to keep going somehow until we reached Solokhumbo. My shoes were completely worn out and torn with walking through the snow."

By this time the frostbite on his feet was so bad that Tashi could not walk any further. The people he was travelling with just cold-heartedly abandoned him and continued on their journey, leaving him behind, totally helpless and in the snow. He could have died!

Tashi continued his story. "I was desperately looking around for a hospital. I was trying to walk, when I met a man who took me to his house nearby. Luckily he was a Tibetan. I called him Akhu which means 'Uncle'. I stayed at his home for a day. Then next day Uncle Nedhon took me to the hospital. There I saw a boy aged about fourteen who had escaped with another group of refugees. He had frostbite all over his body and was so ill, that after two days he died.

"The doctors at the hospital made me put my feet in a bowl of lukewarm water with some yellow medicine in it, to clean them. After that they bandaged my toes. I was in so much pain that I had to ask for something to help me. So they gave me some pills to stop the pain. I stayed in hospital for nine days. After that I felt much better. During my stay in hospital the two European doctors gave me $55 as a donation to help me.

"After I was discharged from the hospital, I stayed at Uncle Nedhon's house for five days. He lived on the ground floor of a two-storied building. On the top was a restaurant. A lot of foreign tourists came there.

Uncle Nedhon took me up to the restaurant, and told my story to the foreigners. They were very kind and collected Rs 3000 (about £60.00 approximately).

"They gave me the money so that I could continue my journey. Uncle Nedhon then asked a Tibetan man who was going to Kathmandu to take me with him as a favour. He agreed, so I went with him. First of all, we had to walk from Solokhumbo to Lukla. We started at 6 am and walked for twelve hours. I had bought a pair of shoes. During the walk I was all right. It was only at the end that I felt pain. I stayed in Lukla for three days with the Tibetan man. Then we took a small aeroplane from Lukla to Kathmandu.

"After reaching Kathmandu, the Tibetan man took me to the Refugee Reception Centre. All the adults from our group had already left but the six children were there. There were three of us boys, Lhakpa, Migmar Tsering and myself, who had very bad frostbite on our feet and toes. We went to the hospital for treatment. After staying there for two weeks, I was well enough to continue my journey. But the other two boys had to stay behind. Later I heard that Migmar had such bad frostbite, that he had to have both his feet amputated - and he was only eight years old!"

Tashi therefore had a very lucky escape. He was able to catch a bus to Delhi, a forty-eight hour journey. After a one night stop, he got a bus to Dharamsala, a twelve hour journey away.

"At last, I arrived here at the Reception Centre. I was very happy to see Dharamsala, and to meet the other children here from Tibet," Tashi finished with a smile.

DANGERS OF ESCAPE

"The younger brother aged ten, witnessed his older brother's murder. The refugees were detained for two days by the Nepalese police and had to pay them everything they had before being released. They then continued their journey to the Refugee Centre at Katmundu.

"There have unfortunately been many cases like this, of refugees who have been killed when travelling through Nepal," Mr Paljor said grimly.

(Below) My first sight of Tashi. He had just returned from hospital, where he had been treated for frost-bite on his feet.

The Tibetan Children's Village

In the early days, in 1959, when His Holiness the Dalai Lama first escaped to India, there were no schools for Tibetan children. At that time so many hundreds of Tibetan children and women died, either of diseases like malaria and TB, or from the hard and dangerous work on road-construction. Their children were left as orphans, without anyone to look after them

It was in 1960 that the Dalai Lama proposed that a centre for orphans and destitute children should be started in Dharamsala. On May 17th 1960, fifty-one children from road-construction camps in Jammu arrived. They were ill and suffering from malnutrition. Mrs Takla, the elder sister of the Dalai Lama volunteered to look after them. The Centre was named the Nursery for Tibetan Refugee Children. Soon children began pouring in from road workers' camps in Kulu, Sikkim, and Nepal.

Gradually news of the Nursery spread, and it began to get support from the international community and from the Government of India. As the numbers of children increased, there was an urgent need for the Nursery to provide educational facilities for the children also. Up to then, children over eight had moved to residential schools in other parts of India, but these now became full to capacity. So in 1971 the Nursery Centre was developed into a school and homes as well.

Today the Tibetan Children's Village in Upper Dharamsala has thirty-three 'Homes'. These are hostels for senior boys and girls, and a separate home for little babies. It is a thriving and successful establishment, with an Infant, Junior and Senior School for children aged from three to twenty years old.

There are very good facilities with sports grounds, a library, science labs, a theatre for music and drama, as well as a splendid temple. The teachers and staff at TCV are mainly former pupils from the school, so they have a tremendous commitment to their teaching, and to the children. As a result, there is a high academic standard, and many children go on to higher education and to university.

The Tibetan Children's Village is unique in that it combines a very good education and also a happy 'Home' life, for those children who are either orphaned, or separated from their parents in Tibet.

The Infant School is for children aged from three to six. The children are taught using the Montessori method, which means that the emphasis is on children learning, rather than the teacher teaching.

The Junior School is for children aged from seven to twelve. The form teacher is responsible for teaching all subjects and each class is divided into sections according to the children's ability.

The Senior School has children aged from thirteen years to young adults of twenty, as some children from Tibet start school later. The various subjects are taught by teachers who are specialists in their field.

In 1986 Tibetan was introduced as the main language for teaching children aged from three to ten. After this English is used as the main language for teaching.

The subjects taught in school include Mathematics, History, Geography, Civics, Economics, Biology, Chemistry, Physics and Hindi. Tibetan is taught as a strong second language, with Tibetan history, religion and folk-tales included in the language course. The children also do drawing and painting.

The entire school, children and staff members alike, are divided into four 'Houses' named after the famous Kings of Tibet: Nyatri, Songtsen, Trisong and Triral.

(Below) Children aged 11-12 in a TCV Junior School.

TCV wants to encourage the all-round development of children, so games and sports are important. Each House has its own team, and games and sports competitions are held between the Houses at various times throughout the year. Soccer, basketball, volleyball, table tennis and throw ball are all popular.

The children belong to the same 'House' throughout their time at TCV. So they have a great loyalty to their House and they take great pride in it. They enjoy taking part in many competitions between the Houses not only in sports, but in debates, drama and poetry recitals, and song and dance competitions.

Tibetan folk dances, songs and music form an important part of life at school. The practice and teaching of Buddhism is also an essential part of their lives. So the children have experience of Tibetan culture and religion, as well as a good academic education at the Tibetan Children's Village.

There are now 2,000 children at TCV in Upper Dharamsala. Most of these children were born in Tibet and had escaped to TCV for their education, as they have no hope in Tibet.

"There is a crisis situation in Tibet now," Mr Khangsar, the Principal of the TCV explained to me. "The Chinese are trying to wipe out the Tibetan culture and identity, and one of the ways to do this is to prevent Tibetan children from having any education…Not only is it almost impossible to get an education beyond the primary level, but when they do go to school, our history has been all messed up, and taught upside down, that 'Tibet is part of China', when Tibet has never been part of China and was independent for 3000 years before the Chinese invasion in 1949!

"The worst part is that the Chinese degrade Tibetans as human beings. The Chinese teachers tell the young Tibetan children, "Your fathers and mothers were serfs and slaves. You are primitive. You have no civilization." This is very shocking to young children who are innocent of everything. They are made to feel inferior to the Chinese and that they are second class citizens.

"Right from the beginning the Chinese put concepts like these into Tibetans' heads. So they never grow up to be proud of being human beings, let alone Tibetan!

"Therefore many parents have become quite desperate and they are either bringing over or sending at least one of their children to India, to be able to get a good education. Huge numbers of children come here unannounced from Tibet. Often they don't just come in ones and twos but they come in groups of fifties and hundreds! That means finding, within the hour, some food and then a place to sleep. We have to fit them into existing classes straightaway. Then maybe start a new class with new teachers. So it's a lot of pressure.

"They come here for a purpose. First, they want to have a formal education, an education that is designed to bring up each child as a Tibetan, who is proud of his or her identity. That is the education they want from here."

(Above) Morning School Assembly at TCV

FUNDING FOR TCVs

The main financial support for the TCV schools come from SOS Kinderdorf International, an aid organisation based in Austria. There are also thousands of benefactors from around the world who sponsor children during their education, as well as many other organisations that give financial help.

(Below) At 'home' - Children doing the washing up after lunch, with their House Mother

Sonam : A Boarder at TCV

(Above) Sonam is standing outside Home No 17 which he shares with fifty other children. They are looked after by a House Mother. Sonam says: "I would like to go back to Tibet when I have finished my studies, to see my parents and the rest of my family."

(Below) Sonam (in foreground) in Class 6 of the TCV chool

Eleven year old Sonam, is a boy now living as a boarder at the Tibetan Children's Village. He told me about his background and about the terrifying experiences that he had witnessing the brutality of Chinese soldiers and police against the Tibetan people in Lhasa.

Sonam talked first about his family life. "I was born in Lhasa. My father's name is Tsewang and my mother's name is Dolma. They have a small family business, sewing hats and bags and handicrafts. They sell their things by the side of the road to people in Lhasa. I also have a younger sister called Nawang, who is ten years old.

"We lived in the Barkhor, in the centre of Lhasa. Our home was a two-storied building, and we lived on the ground floor. When my parents went out to work, I used to stay with my grandparents nearby.

"When I was six, I started going to the Barkhor School. I was learning Tibetan, Chinese, Maths and Science. We had a Tibetan teacher teaching us Chinese, and there were both Tibetan and Chinese teachers teaching different subjects. I enjoyed going to school. But I had to speak Chinese when I lived in Lhasa, in order to be able to speak to the Chinese people in shops and things.

"At the Barkhor there were a lot of Chinese soldiers and Chinese policemen wearing ordinary civilian clothes. I saw three demonstrations taking place in and around the Barkhor in 1990. There were monks and nuns, and other Tibetans, who were taking part in the demonstrations. Some of them were wearing scarves on the lower half of their faces. I was standing in a crowd of people near my home. The monks and nuns, and other demonstrators began shouting: "FREE TIBET! FREE TIBET!" and "TIBET IS AN INDEPENDENT COUNTRY! CHINESE QUIT TIBET!"

"Then the Chinese fired tear-gas into the crowds. I could feel the tear-gas, it was stinging in my eyes. I was really frightened. My parents were not with me but I was with some Tibetan friends. Some of the people who were demonstrating, tried to run away from the Chinese soldiers. But the Chinese chased after them firing tear-gas as they went.

"Then after the demonstration the Chinese were trying to catch people. When we ran to a friend's house, we could hear the Chinese soldiers opening fire. Some bullets came through the door and walls. I saw some Tibetan people who were wounded with bullets in their legs. Some other Tibetans rushed to help them. Thank goodness at that time, no one in my friend's house was caught by the Chinese. But I always had that feeling of fear, with so many Chinese soldiers being there, and the firing and everything.

"Then, not long after this, my parents heard about the good and free education that was being given at TCV in India. They decided it would be better and safer for me to go to India in order to get a good education. So they explained this to me, and said that I would have to stay in India until I had finished my schooling.

"One month after this, I had to leave my parents, my younger sister, and my home in Lhasa. I was of course very upset. I was only nine years old at the time."

Sonam described his escape journey to me. "I came here to India with my grandparents in 1991. We left Lhasa at night-time in a truck. My grandparents had a permit, but I didn't have one. This made things very dangerous for me."

They had to smuggle me out, and I hid under some blankets in the truck. I couldn't breathe properly and I was very scared when the lorry stopped at checkpoints, in case the Chinese should find me. When we reached Dam, my grandparents were allowed to cross over to the next border. As I did not have a permit I was not allowed on the ordinary route. So my grandparents paid some money to a Nepalese couple to take me into Nepal by another route."

Sonam and his cousin Dickyi, had to change into Nepali clothes to disguise themselves. After a short walk, they caught a bus to Kathmandu where the Nepalese couple took them to the Refugee Reception Centre. There, Sonam was overjoyed to meet his grandparents again. They stayed there for a month and then continued their journey by bus, first to Delhi and then up to Dharamsala where at last they reached the Tibetan Children's Village. Sonam was very glad to find so many children there and soon made friends.

Sonam was nine years old when he arrived at TCV. He went to live in Home No 17, with a very nice housemother to look after him, along with a large family of other children. He first joined the Opportunity Class for newly arrived children.

"When I came here to TCV," he said, "it was the first time I had to learn Hindi and English. The teachers here were very good, and we children from Tibet worked very hard, so we were soon able to catch up. What my parents told me was very fresh in my mind. I feel that my parents live a very difficult life under the Chinese. So that is why I study so hard. After one year in the Opportunity Class, I moved up to Class 5. I was the second youngest in my class.

"There are four school houses at TCV, all named after the kings of Tibet. I'm in Nyatri, named after the first king of Tibet. I like my house. In Class 5 most of my subjects were in English. I was learning Tibetan, English, Maths, Social Studies, Science and Hindi - eight subjects altogether, including world Geography. For my exam results I was fourteenth out of thirty-seven pupils. So I was chosen to join the top stream. Now I'm having to learn all the subjects in English - except the Tibetan Language class - of course! My favourite subject is Tibetan literature. I was learning about the different Kings of Tibet and about Buddhism. When I lived in Tibet, my parents were not allowed to practise their religion, because we were living under the Chinese. So coming here, I learnt more about my Buddhist Religion. We have regular prayers in the School

Hall in the mornings and in our Home in the evenings. Every Sunday I go with my friends to the temple, and we walk twenty times around the temple and chorten."

According to Buddhist custom, Tibetans walk clockwise around a temple or holy shrine to show their devotion and respect for the Buddha. It also shows their humility and is a way of dispelling worldly pride.

Finally Sonam told me what he would like to do in the future. "I would like to go back to Tibet when I have finished my studies, to see my parents and my family. Then I would come back here to India to live, until the Chinese have left Tibet. When that day comes, I would like to return to my homeland."

The Principal of TCV, Mr Khangsar told me, "We still have a lot of orphans and destitute children. Many do have parents and are not really orphans. The tragedy is that their parents cannot see them. It takes about ten years for these students to finish school. Then only can they go to see their parents in Tibet - that is if they have the money and the travel permits. In the documents you are required by the Chinese authorities to declare that you are an 'Overseas Chinese' and not a Tibetan. It is a complete robbery of whatever little we have - our identity. But many of our people have done just that, because they haven't seen their loved ones for so long and are willing to risk everything!"

(Right) Sonam visiting the temple at TCV with his House Mother and some friends

Tenzin Wangmo :
A Day Pupil at TCV

(Below) Tenzin Wangmo in the pine forest near McLeod Ganj

Tenzin Wangmo is a twelve year old girl. She is a day pupil at the Tibetan Children's Village and lives in the small town of McLeod Ganj, in Upper Dharamsala. She talked to me about her life both at home and at school, and also about her family background.

"My grandparents, on my father's side, used to live in U-Tsang, in Central Tibet, near Mount Kailash, the sacred Mountain. They were nomads and had big herds of yaks.

"My grandparents escaped from Tibet after the Tibetan Uprising, and the Chinese persecution. They came to India at the same time as His Holiness the Dalai Lama in 1959. My father was only three years old at the time, so he doesn't remember Tibet. My grandmother had twelve children, five of them died when they were little, but five boys and two girls are still alive. Now they have all grown up.

"After arriving in India, my grandparents came to live in Delhi, where they started a small business. Both my parents were able to get a good education, unlike their parents who were illiterate.

My father and mother went to a Central School for Tibetans, run by the Indian Government in Mussoorie. Then my father went on to college and got a degree.

"I was born in Delhi, which is where my parents lived at that time. When I was two months old, my parents brought me to Dharamsala to see His Holiness the Dalai Lama. They asked him to give me a name. He looked into my face, and gave me the name of Tenzin Wangmo. I have one older brother, aged thirteen and two younger sisters. We lived in Delhi until I was four years old. My parents had a small clothes business there. Then my whole family moved to Nainital in Uttar Pradesh. My parents started a new business selling European-style clothes."

Tenzin Wangmo went to three different schools there. When she was five years old, she went to a small Tibetan School, where she was taught in Tibetan. Then at six, she went to a small Indian School where she had to learn Hindi, so she forgot Tibetan. When she was seven, she went to a much bigger Indian School, where there were 1,000 Indian girls and only 3 Tibetans, and all the subjects were taught in English!

"I was nine and a half," Tenzin Wangmo said, "when my parents announced that I should go and live with my grandmother in McLeod Ganj, in Upper Dharamsala, so that I could attend the Tibetan Children's Village School. But they did not explain to me why. It was because they wanted me to have a more Tibetan education and learn my language and about my religion, but I did not know that at the time. My father brought me and my cousin, here to McLeod Ganj to live with my grandmother and uncle in 1990.

"It was really nice for me to find so many Tibetan children at TCV. But I found it very difficult in the beginning, because all the subjects were taught in Tibetan and I had been learning in English. So I had to start learning Tibetan from scratch when I was nine and a half - six years later than the other pupils who had started at three! But I soon caught up with them."

Tenzin Wangmo has now been at TCV for three years. She has not only 'caught up' but is in the top Stream 'A' in the very same Class as Sonam.

MY DAY AT THE TCV

"I have to get up very early at 5.15 every morning. At 5.30am we have our breakfast of milk-tea and bread. Every day after breakfast I visit the temple in McLeod Ganj. I go with my friends, and walk three times around the temple, and spin all the prayer wheels every day before going to school. Then we catch the school bus at 6.00am.

"We start School at 7.00am with prayers to Lord Buddha in the School Hall, followed by Assembly. Then at 7.45am we start our lessons. We finish School at 1.30 in the Summer, as it's very hot. But in Winter we have lessons from 7.30am to 4.00pm, with a break for lunch."

"I'm learning the same subjects as Sonam. My favourite subjects are Maths, Mental Arithmetic, also Science, Social Studies and English. There are thirty-five children in our class and I usually get the highest marks in these subjects.

"At the end of each term we have exams. There are three terms in the year: Term 1 is from March-May; Term 2 is from June-August, and Term 3 is from September-December. So January and February are when we have the main holiday of the year and I go to Nainital to visit my parents, and see my sisters and my brother and friends. We celebrate the Tibetan New Year, Losar, in February. We make new clothes, and paint the house both inside and out. We clean all the things in the house, and throw all the dirty old things away and we get new ones. We also put special colourful decorations in the house. The first day of the Tibetan New Year is the most important. We have to stay near the home. All the children are given money to buy sweets and presents. We have special food during the three days celebrations. We make special deep-fried cakes called 'Khabsays' and meat momo and vegetable momo, many types of momo. We can eat as many sweets as we like! Some people bring sweets from England. We invite our friends and neighbours to our homes and we go to their homes.

"My family drinks 'chang' which is Tibetan beer. Everyone makes chang for Losar, the New Year.

"This is the happiest time of all in the year as I am with my parents and my brother and sisters. My two months holiday seems quite a long time, so I don't mind having to leave my parents, to return to Dharamsala. I am very happy living here with my

grandmother, my uncle and my cousin, who is more like an older brother.

"My uncle works at the Bank every day. He does the shopping in the market, and brings home the vegetables. My grandmother is a very religious person. She goes to the Temple at 5.30 every morning. She prays and meditates all day until 6.00 in the evening and then returns home.

"At the weekends I am allowed to sleep late in the mornings, as I am very tired after getting up so early to go to school. My grandmother makes the breakfast for all of us, with milk-tea, bread and honey. I see my friends in the afternoons. Then in the evenings, about 7.00, I prepare the evening meal for the family. I make rice and a vegetable dish with spices in it. In the evenings we sometimes watch a film on television. Then we eat dinner at 10.00pm, and I go to bed at 10.15 or 10.30.

"When I grow up, I would like to be an air hostess, and travel around the world. First, I would like to visit places in the United States, like San Fransisco, where my aunty lives, also Washington and New York. After that I would like to go to Switzerland where my other aunty works. I would also like to go to England, France and Italy. Then, when I have had a chance to explore the world, only then, would I like to get married and have a family. But that is all too far away for me to think about now."

THE NEED TO RETURN

Ngawang Dorje said, "If we do not get freedom for Tibet during our generation, it will be too late to preserve our identity. By the time our children grow up, having been born in India, they might become open to so many outside influences. They may idealise and look towards the West and aspire to a more materialistic life. They may well forget their main aim of remaining Tibetan and of returning to their homeland.

"I would rather have a small plot of land in Tibet, than all this," as he gestured around the TCV campus with its impressive buildings and community.

(Above) Tenzin Wangmo spins the prayer wheels outside the temple in McLeod Ganj. Religion forms an important part of her life.

Dharamsala :
The Handicraft Centre

Dharamsala is divided into three parts, Lower, Middle and Upper Dharamsala. McLeod Ganj, in Upper Dharamsala, is where the main Tibetan community lives. It is a small town perched high up on the spur of a mountain range in the Himalayas.

Dawa Tsering, the Welfare Officer for Dharamsala, talked to me about both the Tibetan and the Indian communities living there.

"In the beginning, from the 1960's to the mid 1980's, there was not much of a problem with the Indian population. Both the Tibetans and the Indians were honest, uneducated, simple people. The Tibetans came from a rural nomadic or farming background, and the Indian population lived in small villages farming in the mountains surrounding McLeod Ganj. They lived a simple way of life.

"In those early days in the 1960's and 1970's, there were 2,000-3,000 Tibetans living in Dharamsala. But now there are 8,500 Tibetans living here. This covers the whole of Dharamsala and Kangra District, including the two TCV Schools in Upper and Lower Dharamsala.

"In McLeod Ganj alone there are now about 3,600 Tibetans. From the mid 1980's, the changes came from both sides of the communities, both the Indian and the Tibetan. It was at this time that Dharamsala became very famous because of His Holiness the Dalai Lama and the Tibetan community. A lot of foreign tourists started coming. Also the population increased, with more Indian people coming to McLeod Ganj mainly from the Punjab. They mostly had an urban 'street-wise' background and brought in outside influences, which also affected the Tibetan community.

"From the mid 1980's, both sides of the community, the Indian and Tibetan, started up small businesses, shops, hotels and restaurants. This gave rise to jealousy and competition between them.

"However, the majority of the Indian people, that is about 75% of the population, are still living in small villages and farms in the mountains. Others own shops, hotels and restaurants in McLeod Ganj. On the whole, however, the two communities get on very well together.

"Also, if you look at the larger picture of Tibetan settlements in both north and south India, where the majority of 121,000 Tibetan refugees live in exile, both the Government of India, and the Indian people as a whole, have shown enormous generosity and hospitality towards the Tibetan refugees, in providing them with land and facilities to build up their settlements and communities."

THE HANDICRAFT CENTRE

From the 1960's and 1970's Tibetans living in Dharamsala have been mainly dependent on The Handicraft Centre, weaving Tibetan carpets to earn their living. I visited the main Handicraft Centre in McLeod Ganj, where Mrs Thonden, the Manageress, talked to me.

"This Centre is one of the oldest Tibetan Handicraft Centres. We started training people and weaving carpets in 1960, soon after the first wave of Tibetan refugees came over to India with His Holiness the Dalai Lama. So our carpets are well known.

"In Old Tibet both the parents knew how to weave carpets and they would teach their children. Fortunately some skilled carpet weavers came with the early refugees. These craftsmen taught the women how to weave Tibetan carpets. And now those women are teaching the newly arrived female refugees. Today we have nearly 300 people working here.

The people who came early on in 1959 and in the early 1960's left here after their initial training. They built looms in their homes and worked from home.

The refugees who have been coming here since 1980, both men and women, of all ages, are employed by us. We are the biggest employer of Tibetans in McLeod Ganj and especially for newly arrived refugees.

The Reception Centre are sending me many refugees from Tibet. Sometimes twenty, sometimes ten, will all arrive at once. And they need food and somewhere to live and they bring their children with them. They come and they say: 'We have no food, no clothes, no way of earning our living. Please can you help us?' So I have to find them accommodation and organise the education of their children, and provide for their clothes and their food. So I am like the mother of a hundred children!"

"The Tibetan families who came in the 1960's had six or seven children. But recent refugees only have one or two children, as the Chinese have had a strict policy of one child per family, which forced many women to have abortions and sterilisations.

"Most of the blocks of flats in McLeod Ganj belong to the Handicraft Centre. So we are able to provide free accommodation for the people who work here.

Many Tibetans who come here don't know anything. They have had no education and are illiterate. We give them training for six months to learn carpet weaving. It is the women and girls who are weaving the carpets. For the men, we give them six months training to do carpet trimming. We also have a Tailoring Section, consisting mainly of men, and a few women. It is a one year training course."

I also spoke to Dolma, aged twenty-eight, who had escaped to India in 1988. She described how she had learnt to weave carpets. "I started by learning how to thread the loom, then how to make knots in the carpet and how to follow the design step by step. There are eight knots per square on the chart. Therefore I keep that in my head, whilst weaving and looking at the design on the chart. This is the most difficult part. It took me a couple of months to learn how to weave carpets. I worked on a small carpet with another weaver who showed me how to do it. I hope to earn enough, so I can send some money back to help my family in Tibet."

To weave a carpet 1m x 2m takes a woman fifteen to twenty days. In one month she can make almost two carpets. So a woman can earn Rs1,000 in a month, which is about £20.00.

Mrs Thonden described how the carpets are sold. "We have a Handicraft Shop here. We do some selling from our Showroom. But we sell most of our carpets for export around the world."

(Above) Two women working at a loom weaving a Tibetan carpet, at the Handicraft Centre. Making and selling carpets provides the main economic support for the Tibetan community.

(Below) Men trimming carpets at the Handicraft Centre

(Far Left on page 26) A woman working on a single loom, watched by her child. Many women at the Handicraft Centre have babies who are cared for in the splendid new Baby Room.

The Norbulingka Arts Centre and the Master Thangka Painter

The Norbulingka Institute was founded by the Department of Religious and Cultural Affairs in 1989, to help to preserve Tibetan Art and Culture in exile. It is named after the Dalai Lama's Summer Palace in Lhasa in Tibet.

I went to the Art Centre at Norbulingka to see how Thangka Painting is being taught, and to talk to Tempa, the Master Painter there. He was just putting the finishing touches of gold to a beautiful painting showing Tsong Khapa and the Gelugpa Refuge Tree.

Tempa put down his brush and talked to me about his training and work. "I am Master of the Thangka Painting School here at Norbulingka. I did my training in Tibet. I was living in Lhasa and learned from a monk there. He was a Master Thangka Painter but he had to keep it secret. He could not wear monk's robes and he had to work as a servant for the Chinese, doing menial jobs, like carrying water. Nobody knew that he was a

(Left) The Master Thangka painter, Tempa at work

(Far left on page 28) The God of Anger, a Thangka painting by Tempa

Master Painter. It was in fact very dangerous to be doing Thangka Painting.

"This is a sacred art which the Tibetans use for religious purposes. The Chinese do not allow Tibetans to practise their religion or do Thangka Painting. So both the monk and I could have been arrested and imprisoned, if we had been found out. I used to go to my teacher's house in the mornings and in the evenings to do the painting in secret. I was twelve years old when I started, and it took me seven years of training to learn Thangka painting. I also started training as an apprentice from the age of twelve, working with teams of Tibetan painters who were restoring the murals in the Jokhang temple. They had been damaged during the Cultural Revolution." The Chinese wanted the paintings to be restored, so that visiting tourists would see them, and think that there was freedom of religion again in Tibet, but this was only a facade.

"I came to India to see my relatives in 1985 and I decided to stay here. It was in 1989 that I came to the Norbulingka, and started the Thangka Painting School here. There are now ten painters who have completed their training, and who are now working on paintings commissioned from outside. I have four students at present, two monks and two teenage boys.

"First of all, I have to teach them the sacred texts and scripts that lay down the proportions of the Thangka Paintings. It takes five to six years to learn drawing and painting under a Master, before one can work independently.

"I was asked by His Holiness the Dalai Lama to do this huge Thangka painting of Palchen Dorje Shonu. He is the God of Anger, for the Nyingmapa Sect. It took me almost two years to complete, as I am also overseeing the building work here. It is my job to make sure that the woodcarving, painting and decoration are done in the fine Tibetan tradition."

When I first visited the Norbulingka Art Centre in 1993, it was still under construction, and the temple was just an architect's drawing on a piece of paper. On my return two years later, I was amazed to see that the temple was completed. It is a magnificent building, maintaining the Tibetan architectural style. The painting and decoration of the inside of the temple was being carried out by groups of Tibetan artists who had been trained by Tempa. Golden Buddhas, Gods and flowers flowed from their brushes. It was a revelation to see.

MONASTERIES IN TIBET

For over a thousand years Buddhism flourished in Tibet. During that time it was the monasteries which were the treasure houses of art and scriptures, and which contained the cultural heritage of Buddhism in Tibet.

Following the Chinese invasion in 1950, almost all of the 6000 monasteries were destroyed. Today only parts of thirteen monasteries remain. The Chinese carried out a systematic destruction of the monasteries. First special teams of mineralogists removed all the precious stones such as rubies, emeralds, turquoise and lapiz lazuli which decorated the beautiful statues. Then teams of metallurgists graded the statues according to the metals they were made of, such as gold, silver and bronze. Everything of value was loaded onto trucks and sent to China. There the sacred statues of gold and silver were melted down for bullion or sold on the international art market. Finally the Chinese blew up the walls of the monasteries with dynamite. As well as looting all the treasures the Chinese burnt millions of religious books.

Namgyal Monastery: Saka Dawa and the Kalachakra Teachings

For Tibetans, one of the most important aspects of their lives is their Buddhist religion. It gives them joy and inspiration and has helped them to overcome their suffering, and to rebuild their lives in exile.

At the heart of the Tibetan community is the monastery, where the Buddhist monks live, and where people come to worship. In Old Tibet the monasteries were the main centres of learning, art, culture and religion. There were about 6,000 monasteries in Tibet, before they were almost all destroyed by the Chinese between 1959 to 1961.

Only a few monks managed to escape from the terrible Chinese persecution, and follow the Dalai Lama to India in 1959. When they first arrived they lived in refugee camps in Missamari, Buxa Duar and Dalhousie, where they experienced extreme hardship.

Gradually, over the years, the Tibetan community in exile has been able to build many new monasteries. Sera, Ganden and Drepung are the biggest monasteries in South India. But it is Namgyal Monastery, where the Dalai Lama has his residence, in Upper Dharamsala, that is the heart of the Tibetan community. Many hundreds of Tibetans, both living in exile and in Tibet, make the pilgrimage to the temple in Namgyal Monastery to see the Dalai Lama, and receive his blessing.

Today there are about 180 monks living in Namgyal Monastery. They belong to the Gelugpa, the 'Yellow Hat' School. They offer religious service to Tenzin Gyatso, the Fourteenth Dalai Lama, just as the monks did in the past to the Great Fifth Dalai Lama in the 17th century.

It is here at the temple in Namgyal Monastery that the main religious festivals are celebrated. Saka Dawa is one of the most important religious festivals in the year. It celebrates the Birth, Enlightenment and Death of the Buddha. I was very fortunate to be in Dharamsala on June 4th for Saka Dawa, the Buddha Day.

The ceremony started in the temple at Namgyal Monastery in the dark early hours of the morning. The Dalai Lama administered the Precepts from 4.00am-6.00am to hundreds of people, who had travelled through the night for the ceremony.

I arrived at the Monastery at 6.30am when the sun was up. It was crowded with people. A huge Thangka picture of Lord Buddha, about 50 feet or 16 metres high, was hanging facing the entrance of the temple.

The expression of the Buddha was peaceful and smiling. He was sitting in the lotus position, with his hands in the teaching mudra. The early morning sun shone in a bright shaft of light across his face. Arranged in front of him were tables covered with hundreds of gold-flamed butter lamps, which were being tended by the monks in their dark red and gold robes. It was one of the most beautiful sights that I have ever seen.

Hundreds of people, both Tibetans and Indians, came to the temple. They began with circum-nambulations (walking around the temple several times), and spinning the prayer wheels as they passed. Then they visited the shrine of the Buddha, and offered white silk scarves called 'katas'. They said prayers and donated money for the Monastery. Then they sat in front of the temple to watch and listen to the monks chanting sacred texts, playing music, and carrying out sacred rituals and ceremonies for many hours. The ceremony lasted until 6.00pm. Then it was time to go home. It was a wonderful and memorable day.

THE KALACHAKRA TEACHINGS

It was 2,500 years ago that the Buddha gave the first Kalachakra teachings in India. These teachings went from India to Tibet in the 11th Century. It is only in Tibet that these teachings, the Highest Yoga Tantras, were preserved and practised after the decline of Buddhism in India. Since then, the teachings have been transmitted in an unbroken lineage from teacher to disciple.

Today the monks at Namgyal Monastery still continue to practise the Kalachakra teachings and ceremonies. The Fire Puja Ritual, which is the final part of the Kalachakra Ceremony, was explained to me by a monk. "We burn ritual offerings called 'Jin Seg'. There are ten different substances for the Fire Puja - rice to help people to increase their health, dhruva grass to help to achieve long life, and melted butter to help to achieve enlightenment. When we perform the Fire Puja, we have to transform all those substances into Great Bliss and Wisdom."

The Ritual Master who led the ceremony was Venerable Thupten Chogden. He is now in his late 70's. He was the Chanting Master in Old Tibet. He was imprisoned by the Chinese for twenty years and only came over to India in 1985. Now he is able to teach the younger monks how the Highest Tantric Rituals should be practised, and thus keep alive this unique and important tradition.

(Far left on page 30) A Thangka picture of Lord Buddha. This 16th Century wall hanging was rescued from Tibet in 1959 and now forms the centre of worship for Saka Dawa, the Buddha Day.

(Overpage on page 32-33) Monks from Namgyal Monastery performing the Fire Puja Ritual

Gedhun Choekyi Nyima:
The true Reincarnation of The Tenth Panchen Lama

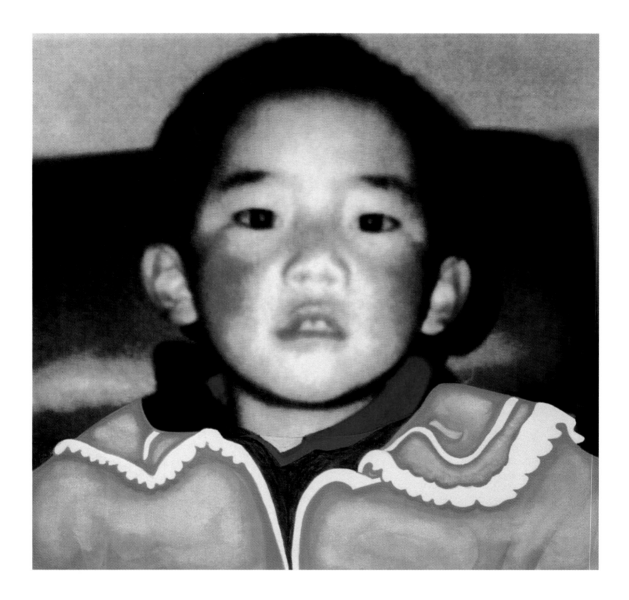

I was visiting the Department of Information and International Relations in Dharamsala when I heard the exciting news. It was 14th May 1995 when His Holiness the Dalai Lama made the announcement that he had recognised the six year old boy, Gedhun Choekyi Nyima as the reincarnation of the tenth Panchen Lama who had died on 28th January 1989. The news was greeted with grand religious offerings and public celebrations in Tibetan communities all over India.

The little boy, Gedhun Choekyi Nyima, was born on 25th April 1989 to a poor nomad family living in the Lhari District of Nagchu on the remote and freezing high plateau in Northern Tibet. It is not unusual in Tibet, as in the Panchen Lama's case, to find that the reincarnated Lama has returned as the son of simple yak-herders or farmers who are devout Buddhists.

The Panchen Lama is the second most important spiritual leader in Tibet after the Dalai Lama. Although there has sometimes been

Gedhun Choekyi Nyima: The true Reincarnation of The Tenth Panchen Lama

rivalry between the Dalai Lama's throne in Lhasa and the Panchen Lama's in Shigatse, the present Dalai Lama was apparently on very friendly terms with the last Panchen Lama. Soon after the tenth Panchen Lama died, the Dalai Lama's government-in-exile requested that senior monks be allowed into Tibet to search for his successor. The Chinese refused and instead launched their own quest for the new Panchen Lama. The Chinese authorities knew that if they controlled the new Panchen Lama they would be able not only to manipulate him for their purposes but also to control the selection of the 15th Dalai Lama after the death of the current Dalai Lama.

The Chinese search party consisted of Chinese officials, who as Communists, did not have any strong Buddhist beliefs and did not know about divinations or the religious rituals that were needed to find a new reincarnate. So to help them and to speed things up, they included in their search party, several lamas from the Panchen Lama's monastery, Tashilhumpo. The lama in charge of the search party, Chatrel Rinpoche, was the abbot of the monastery.

Meanwhile, the Dalai Lama was pursuing his own investigations from India, helped by many lamas from Tashilhumpo who had escaped from Tibet. The number of boys who were possible candidates kept growing. Some were in Tibet, others among the Tibetan refugee communities scattered throughout India. Then came a breakthrough. Investigations by both the Dalai Lama and Chatrel Rinpoche were leading to the same six year old nomad boy in Nagchu Prefecture. The child had been shown possessions belonging to the late Panchen Lama which he identified correctly. Also, his birthplace matched discriptions given to the Dalai Lama by several of Tibet's protected oracles - men who enter trances and allow the spirit of a diety to speak through them. As the final test, the Dalai Lama wrapped the names of all thirty candidates inside dough balls and mixed them up. One witness said, "The ball with Gedhun's name seemed to fly up at the Dalai Lama not once but several times. The Dalai Lama laughed and said, 'It's just like magic!'"

When the Dalai Lama announced his selection of the new Panchen Lama on 14th May 1995, the Chinese were furious. They immediately acted. They swooped down on the nomad encampment and kidnapped the young boy and his parents. It is thought that Gedhun and his parents are being kept prisoners somewhere in Beijing.

The Chinese anger at being outwitted by the Dalai Lama has fallen most heavily on Chatrel Rinpoche. He was arrested on 14th May 1995 and sent to Beijing where he was kept in solitary confinement. The Chinese put heavy pressure on him to denounce Gedhun but he refused to do so.

Later in May, Tashilhumpo Monastery was surrounded by more than a thousand Chinese soldiers armed with assault rifles. Inside the Monastery, monks were forced to sign documents denouncing their former abbot, Chatrel Rinpoche and the new Panchen Lama.

In December 1995 the Chinese authorities chose another six year old Tibetan boy as the reincarnation of the Panchen Lama. He was enthroned on 8th December at Tashilhumpo Monastery. The news was greeted with anger by the Tibetan people who denounced Beijing's enthronment of this rival Panchen Lama. No Tibetan, either in exile or in Tibet, accepted or will accept the Chinese choice of the rival Panchen Lama.

The Chinese have insisted on their choice so that they can brainwash and manipulate him as their puppet to oppose the present Dalai Lama. There would also be the possibility of his choosing the next Dalai Lama who would then be a figurehead under the control of Chinese government.

By putting their own candidate as the new Panchen Lama, the Chinese are trying to divide the Tibetan people and destroy their religion and culture.

Today, Gedhun Choekyi Nyima is still being held under house arrest. No one knows where he is being kept in China and at the age of nine, Gedhun Choekyi Nyima is the youngest political prisoner in the world.

Reincarnation

Buddhist believe that after a person dies, he or she will be reborn. This is called reincarnation.

A person is reborn according to their karma. If a person has been good and caring, they will have good karma and will be reborn as a human being. But if a person has been selfish, cruel or evil, they will have bad karma and will be reborn as a lower species. Tibetan monks lead very good lives, teaching the Buddha Dharma, and helping people. When a High Lama dies he will always have a reincarnation as a baby boy, called a Tulku, who in turn grows up to be a good and wise lama. In Old Tibet there were several thousand tulkus and every monastery had its tulku. After the Chinese invaded Tibet they drove the monks out of the monasteries, forced many into labour camps or killed them. During this time many tulkus were lost or died. Some however were able to escape to Nepal and India.

(Far left on page 34) Gedhun Choekyi Nyima (aged 6), the true reincarnation of the Tenth Panchen Lama. He was discovered by the Dalai Lama on 14th May 1995.

The Tibet Support Workshop

TIBET'S INDEPENDENCE

The Dalai Lama said, "I want to share with you my strong feelings and anxiety on some urgent matters of the present time. Recent scientific studies of archeological findings have revealed that the Tibetans and Chinese have been two distinct peoples since the dawn of human civilisation. There is clear evidence that the genesis of civilisations in China, Tibet and India are different. Based on this, the distinct existance of the Tibetan race is clear. For example in the 7th and 8th Centuries Tibet was a mighty kingdom in Central Asia."

(Below) A crowd greeting the Dalai Lama as he arrived for the Tibet Support Workshop

It was 9.30 in the morning, and already the sun was hot overhead. I was standing amongst a crowd of Tibetan men, women and children who were gathered outside the 'Kashag' building of the Tibetan Government-in-Exile. They had been waiting patiently for over an hour. People were holding flowers and incense sticks, or katas, in their hands. Parents held babies and young children in their arms, offering flowers. Suddenly the crowd moved eagerly forward. A white limousine slowly came into view, stopping near the steps. His Holiness the Dalai Lama stepped out, smiling at the people to acknowledge their greetings. Then he turned, and went up the steps to the Kashag building.

It was Sunday May 30th 1993 and the Dalai Lama had come to speak to the delegates attending a Support for Tibet Workshop organised by the Committee for Solidarity with the Tibet Liberation Movement in Dharamsala. Attending the meeting were Indian politicians, defence specialists, academics, journalists and senior Tibetan Ministers.

The Dalai Lama gave the opening address.

"Today, our friends from the Sublime Land of India, with whom the Snow Land of Tibet enjoys a teacher-pupil relationship, have come here, out of a sense of responsibility, to speak on and discuss the issue of Tibet.

"India and Tibet have unique relations. If we look at past history, our culture and religion, which are renowned in the world for their richness, they came from India. Similarly our tradition of non-violence came from India.

"During the past thirty-four years, India has been our second home. The Government of India, the host State Governments and particularly the local Indian people, with whom we have come into contact, have been very close to us, and treated us as members of their family. We are not the only refugees. There are other refugees as well. But the kind of attitude of our hosts makes us feel as if we are in our own homeland.

"The present crisis, as I see it, is the danger of Tibet being converted into a veritable Chinese land. One of the key threats is the transfer of Chinese settlers there. Ever since the Chinese invaded Tibet in 1949, they have been bringing in millions of Chinese settlers into Tibet.

"There are now 7.5 million Chinese people living in Tibet and 6 million Tibetans. This is endangering the survival of Tibetan people. Yet the 'Population Transfer Programme', as it is called, is now being stepped up by the Chinese authorities."

The Dalai Lama said that Tibet must be liberated before the Chinese Government succeeded in completely destroying the Tibetan people's identity and their culture, through its carefully planned 'demographic invasion' of bringing in more and more millions of Chinese people into Tibet. He also said that freedom for Tibet would be meaningless if it came after Tibetans had been reduced to a minority in their own country, its cultural heritage and its environment destroyed, and its natural resources exhausted.

"Time is running out for the Tibetans. The Chinese are working overtime to wipe out the Tibetan identity. It is not merely an issue of liberating the homeland of the Tibetans, but a global issue." He said that the complete changes that China was aiming for, would have serious political, military, and environmental repercussions on the entire world.

Asian countries like India would be directly affected. A "free Tibet" would not serve as a buffer zone between India and China if the Chinese population were in the majority there.

Similarly, the fact that the Chinese were dumping nuclear waste in Tibet was causing a major threat of pollution to all downhill countries like India, Bangladesh and others, which have rivers running through them whose sources are in Tibet.

The Dalai Lama then turned to the issue of the Chinese abuse of Human Rights in Tibet. He said that the Chinese have used methods of force and fear to control the Tibetan people, but have so far failed to win the people over.

"The Tibetan national spirit is alive," he said and he went on to explain that the young men and women of Tibet today, had turned in deadly hatred against the Chinese, as they killed and tortured hundreds of Tibetans during the Demonstration supporting Tibetan Independence in 1989, and continue to do so still.

The Dalai Lama said that he would however not support a violent struggle against the Chinese. "If the Tibetan youth decides to take up the course of violence, then I will resign and stop leading the movement. Non-violence is crucial…as even after liberation, Tibet and China would have to co-exist like good neighbours."

His Holiness concluded: "It is necessary to save Tibet. But it is also necessary to be realistic. The essence of my idea so far has been to halt the transfer of Chinese population into Tibet, and gradually convert the whole of Tibet into a zone of peace and non-violence. There is an urgent need for this."

The Support for Tibet Workshop had been opened the previous day by George Fernandes MP. He said that the world could not turn a blind eye to the happenings in Tibet. A whole race was being wiped out, the entire Himalayan environment was being threatened because of large-scale deforestation and the dumping of nuclear waste; and the Roof of the World was being converted into a launching pad for delivering nuclear warheads on Asian targets.

Tashi Wangdi, Minister for International Affairs in the Government-in-exile, suggested that India and other countries should review their policy on Tibet, and support the Resolution on Tibet at the next United Nations Commission on Human Rights.

(Below) The Dalai Lama with Indian delegates after the Tibet Support Workshop

TIBET'S INDEPENDENCE
(continued)

"China claims that Tibet became part of its empire in the 13th Century. However, Tibetan historical documents of different periods, only show the existance of the priest-patron relationship between Tibet and China. Even in the later centuries, when the Manchu Emperors gained strong influence in Tibet, the relationship between the two nations was viewed only in terms of priest-patron and not in any other light…Also there is no record of taxes being paid to the Chinese by the Tibetans.

"Therefore historically Tibet was a completely independent nation. Likewise international legal experts contend that Tibet was a de facto independent nation before the Chinese invasion."

Dolma Ling Nunnery

(Above) Nuns from the Dolma Ling Nunnery. Sangmo, the senior nun, is in the middle of the back row. Ngawang is on the far right of the back row.

Since the Chinese occupation of Tibet in 1950, the policy of the Chinese authorities has been to destroy the monasteries and the Tibetan religion and culture. Hundreds of Tibetans still suffer from persecution at the hands of the Chinese. Many Tibetans, including monks and nuns and people of all ages, continue to risk their lives escaping from Tibet to the safety and freedom of India.

It was in early 1991 that large numbers of refugee nuns began arriving in Dharamsala, having escaped from Tibet. About 200 nuns arrived in that year alone. One group of about 60 nuns spent two years on a pilgrimage from Lithang, in Kham in Eastern Tibet, doing prostrations all the way to Lhasa, to visit the Jokhang temple. But the Chinese authorities would not allow them to enter Lhasa. So they fled to India.

Many of the nuns who arrived came from the Lhasa area. It was in 1989 in Lhasa, that many brave monks and nuns took leadership roles against the Chinese. After arresting them, many of the nuns were imprisoned and tortured.The Chinese were particularly brutal to them.

The Chinese authorities also closed down the nunneries and made it illegal for the nuns to practise their religion. Many nuns fled to India. After enduring a difficult and dangerous journey over the Himalayas, they arrived in Dharamsala, with nothing but the clothes that they stood up in; to a community which was already seriously overcrowded with existing resources severely overstretched with the huge influx of new refugees.

The Tibetan Nuns Project, formed in 1987, was supported by the Tibetan Women's Association and the Department of Religion and Culture. The Tibetan Nuns Project arranged for help from the community for the immediate needs of the nuns. They organised a sponsorship programme, appealing to friends all over the world for funds to help the nuns. Enough funds were raised to pay for the basic needs of shelter, food, health care and the beginning of an educational programme for the nuns.

In August 1992 the Tibetan Nuns Project bought a four acre plot of land in the Kangra valley below Dharamsala. This was to be the site of the new nunnery called Dolma Ling. It was to be designed in the Tibetan architectural style. The plan provided for a nunnery for 200 nuns, with an Institute of Higher Buddhist Studies. The building plan was broken down into two phases, so that building construction could start, even before all the necessary funds were raised. The nuns were also going to help with building the nunnery, to keep costs as low as possible. Temporary living quarters were found for over 100 nuns, in a farmhouse near the site of the nunnery.

I visited the nuns many times during May and June 1993. They lived in cramped and primitive conditions, with no bathroom or sanitation. They had to wash out of doors in the streams. The kitchen was a lean-to, with huge metal cooking pots on open fires. Their 'temple' was improvised with a canvas roof.

Despite these difficult conditions, the nuns continued to follow the strict routine and discipline of a nunnery. They were following the religious practise, of prayer, chanting and education. The new nunnery of Dolma Ling had thus been created even before the nuns had their actual building, through their great faith, courage and determination.

Sangmo, the senior nun in charge, said in 1993, "The living conditions here are nothing compared with what I have been through in Tibet. What matters is that now our nunnery is recognised, and we can practise our religion together without fear. We come from different areas of Tibet. Now that we are a recognised nunnery, it gives us a lot of pride and a sense of achievement."

At last in July 1994 the nuns were able to move into the new buildings of the Dolma Ling Nunnery.

Ngawang's Story

During my visits to Dolma Ling Nunnery in May and June, I became friends with a nun named Ngawang. She talked to me about her life.

"I am 22 years old. I was born in Meldro Gungkar near Lhasa in U-Tsang Province. My father was a farmer. I have two sisters and one brother, who is a monk. When I was a child I helped my parents working in the fields. I only had one year at school. When I was twelve, I went to live with my uncle in Lhasa, as he had no children. He was a Thangka painter. I was not able to go to school there either, so I just did chores around the house. My father died when I was fifteen and my mother died about a year ago.

"When I was very young, I thought that I would like to be a nun. When I reached the age of eighteen, I felt that it was time for me to become a nun. So I asked one of my uncle's friends to find me a place in a nunnery.

"I was admitted to Chusang Nunnery near Lhasa and was ordained by Gyaltsen Shakya, the High Lama from Sera Monastery. I was there for only six months.

"Soon after I arrived at Chusang, in 1989, I saw a big demonstration led by monks and nuns in Lhasa. The Chinese opened fire and killed twenty people. I almost got killed but I managed to escape that time.

"Just after this, eight nuns from our nunnery, including myself, met three monks from Bharlogu. We decided to hold our own demonstration later, in August 1989, on the day of the Shoton Festival. On that day, crowds of people had come to picnic in the park near the Norbulingka Palace and to watch the masked dances. There were lots of Chinese soldiers around watching everything.

"While the people were performing the masked dances, we met up with the three monks. We walked three times around the stage demonstrating. We shouted: "TIBET IS A FREE COUNTRY!" and "CHINA SHOULD QUIT TIBET!" Then we climbed up on the stage and walked around shouting: "HIS HOLINESS THE DALAI LAMA IS OUR SOLE LEADER!" As we tried to leave the park all of us nuns were caught by the Chinese soldiers, but the monks managed to escape. We were handcuffed and put in a lorry. The Chinese soldiers beat us with belts, and kicked us endlessly.

"When we reached the prison, the soldiers took each nun into a different room. I was put in a cell by myself, still handcuffed. For one month I was interrogated every day in a room by four soldiers. They asked me for the names of the leaders of our demonstration. But I never gave away the names of the monks. The soldiers said

to me, 'You will never gain your Independence, so it is no use demonstrating.' I replied, 'Until we gain our freedom, there is no other way for us, except to take to the streets and demonstrate.' Then the soldiers pushed me up against the wall, between the table and a wall, and they beat me with chains around my head and body. They put an electric prod in my mouth and on my face. It sent shocks through me. But I remained silent. However much we were tortured, we did not give away the names of the monks."

Ngawang was imprisoned for two years in Gutsa prison and spent the last three months in hospital. When she was released, she found that she had been expelled from the nunnery. Soon afterwards, she decided to escape to India. She arrived in Dharamsala in 1991 and joined the nuns of Dolma Ling. By July 1994, Ngawang and the other nuns moved into the new Dolma Ling Nunnery.

(Below) Ngawang, the brave young nun, who was imprisoned and tortured by the Chinese

Tashi: My Adopted Son

(Above) Tashi and I at the top of Tashi Choeling Monastery, where I was living. It became Tashi's second home.

I first met Tashi on Wednesday, 16th June 1993 at the Refugee Reception Centre, where I was interviewing him, with the help of an interpreter. Tashi had just told me the harrowing story of his escape from Tibet over the Himalayas to India, which is described earlier.

At the very end of the interview, I asked Tashi if he had any questions that he would like to ask me. He said, "Please, kindly look for a sponsor for me for my school. I have heard about the need for a sponsor, from other children from TCV." So I said that I would try to find one on my return to England, and I continued with my other interviews.

It was only later that evening, after work, when I had time to think about it, that I realised that - Yes - I would like to be Tashi's sponsor! I thought about it carefully, knowing that it would be quite a responsibility to help fund Tashi at school, and possibly college, for maybe the next ten years. But yes - I could do it.

Early on Friday morning, I went to the office at the Reception Centre to see Mr Yulgyal, the Deputy Head, to discuss my decision. He was very pleased and sent someone to fetch Tashi. When I told him that I would like to be his sponsor, Tashi's face lit up in a big smile. He looked delighted, and thanked me very much.

The first thing was to take Tashi by taxi up the mountain to the TCV to meet Miss Dolma, the Sponsorship Secretary and Mr Pasang, the Admissions Officer, to make my sponsorship official, and to introduce Tashi to them. I hoped that he would be able to go to this main TCV school, as it had all the facilities. But it was unlikely, as it was very full already.

The next thing was to buy Tashi the basic school equipment that he needed: a pencil box, pencils, pens, a ruler, eraser, some exercise books and a drawing pad. He was very pleased.

Then we walked past the little Tibetan shops full of exotic jewellery, antiques, bags and clothes, down the road back to the Reception Centre and to the dormitory. It was time for Tashi to return.

The dormitory was a huge room, very dark and crowded with refugees - men, women and children. There seemed to be at least a hundred people there, with several people on each bed; some with a family sleeping, or young men playing cards, or people eating bowls of food. The place stank of rotting rice and dirty, sweaty unwashed bodies. The wooden beds were crammed together in rows. Tashi's bed was at the far end of the dormitory. I must say that I felt quite upset at having to leave him there in these dirty, squalid conditions. But he had to stay there, with the other children, until it was his turn to go to one of the TCV schools. From then on I decided to help Tashi as much as I could, to take him out, and to spend time with him.

Tashi Choeling Monastery Guest House, where I was staying, became like a home for Tashi. He would come regularly to see me there and have a good wash in my little bathroom. Then he would sit comfortably and read some of the Tibetan children's story books, that I had bought him. Sometimes, he would draw or write the Tibetan script.

I took Tashi for regular meals to the Ladies' Venture Restaurant nearby. His favourite dish was the Tibetan Mutton Noodle Soup with vegetables, more like a stew. He would eat this with a pair of chopsticks, with a speed and dexterity that was astounding!

Tashi did not know his way about at all when I first met him, so it was fun taking him to places. I shall never forget the first time we visited the Lingkor. We walked around the path and Tashi pointed out the sacred mantra carved on the mani stones - OM MANI PADME HUM - which means *The Jewel in the Lotus*. After that we went for many walks up and down the mountain to visit the big monasteries, Namgyal or Nechung.

Tashi could walk quite well, but he still had to go to the Clinic in McLeod Ganj for regular treatment for the frost-bite wounds on his foot.

We also went on several epic shopping expeditions to get Tashi kitted out with all the clothes that he needed for school: shirts, underwear, trousers, a new pair of sandals, a travelling bag, and a silver coloured metal trunk.

We had several false starts with Tashi getting all ready to go to the TCV School, only to be told that the new TCV was not ready yet.

Then, at last, on Monday July 12th the *Great Day* arrived for Tashi to go to the Tibetan Children's Village School. I went with him on the bus, along with twenty-five other refugee children. After a three hour journey we reached the new TCV School near Bir. Soon after we arrived, there was a small ceremony to inaugurate the new school, and speeches were made to welcome the children. After lunch, I helped Tashi to arrange his clothes in the trunk in his dormitory. It was new and clean, with good bunk beds. I also met Tashi's House Mother, a very kind woman. Only too soon it was time to say *Goodbye* to darling Tashi, my adopted son, and to leave him in his new home.

NEWS OF TASHI

During the last three years I have been in regular contact with Tashi, through an exchange of letters.

Tashi found it difficult at first to settle down to the routine and discipline of school. With the love and support of his House Mother and teachers, he began working hard in class and getting on well with everyone.

I was thrilled to get his letter in which he wrote:

My dearest Mother Carol

I received your letter and feel as if I am talking in front of you. I am very happy here, so don't worry about me. I am doing well at my studies and giving respect to my teachers and friendly with all. I am also keeping in touch with my parents in Tibet.

Your loving son
Tashi

(Left) Tashi with a mani (prayer) stone, when we visited the Lingkor

Tibet Independence Day Around the World

Every year on March 10th His Holiness the Dalai Lama makes an important speech to mark the anniversary of the Tibetan Uprising in March 1959. These are some extracts from his 1997 speech.

"In the closing years of the 20th Century as we commemorate the thirty-eighth anniversary of the Tibetan Peoples' National Uprising, it is evident that the human community has reached a critical juncture in its history. The world is becoming smaller and increasingly interdependent. One nation's problem can no longer be solved by itself. Without a sense of universal responsibility our very future is in danger...

"As we commemorate this anniversary, we look back at yet another year of escalating repression in Tibet, where the Chinese authorities continue to commit widespread and grave human rights abuses..."

These are some of the worsening conditions for Tibetans living inside Tibet today:

· Increasing numbers of Tibetans are being imprisoned and tortured by the Chinese, for their peaceful resistance to the Chinese occupation of their country. Many Tibetans have died.

· Hundreds of monks and nuns have been expelled from their monasteries and nunneries in Tibet as a result of the Chinese political re-education programme forced upon them. Many of them have been imprisoned while others are risking their lives escaping over the high passes of the Himalayas to India.

· Tibetan children are unable to get any education after primary school. Most Tibetans in Tibet are illiterate.

· There is no employment for Tibetans except hard manual jobs. All good jobs are taken by the Chinese.

· Millions of Chinese settlers continue to move into Tibet under China's Population Transfer Programme. There are now 7.5 million Chinese and only 6 million Tibetans living in Tibet. The Tibetans are now a minority in their own country and their identity is being destroyed.

· Thousands of Tibetan women are forced to have abortions or be sterilised after the birth of one child.

· Tibetans are not allowed to practise their religion.

· Tibet's environment is being destroyed. The Chinese have already cut down forty percent of Tibet's forests and are now mining extensively.

· Tibet is used by the Chinese as a nuclear missile base. They are dumping nuclear waste in Tibet, with severe repercussions for Central Asia.

His Holiness the Dalai Lama continued his speech:

"These new measures in the field of culture, religion and education, coupled with the unabated influx of Chinese immigrants to Tibet, which has the effect of overwhelming Tibet's distinct culture and religious identity and reducing the Tibetans to an insignificant minority in their own country, amount to a policy of cultural genocide...If this population transfer is allowed to continue, in a few decades the Tibetan civilisation will cease to exist.

"I will continue to counsel for non-violence, but unless the Chinese authorities forsake the brutal methods they employ, it will be difficult to prevent the situation in Tibet from deteriorating further..."

As His Holiness the Dalai Lama says, "Time is running out for the Tibetans." We in the West can influence changes. We need to put economic and political pressure on China to free Tibet, before it's too late and the Tibetan civilisation is lost forever.

TIBET DAY: FROM DHARAMSALA TO LONDON, PARIS, NEW YORK & JAPAN

In Dharamsala, the Dalai Lama addressed a crowd of thousands of Tibetans and Indian supporters.

In Switzerland 2000 Tibetans and Human Rights activists from across Europe demonstrated in front of the United Nations headquarters in Geneva.

In Ottawa (Canada) 100 people protested. In New York around 500 Tibetans and their supporters marched to the Chinese UN Mission. Demonstrations were held in other cities in the United States.

(Below) A Tibetan monk with Tibetans and their supporters demonstrating outside the Foreign Office in London

Glossary

Communism: A political and economic system which advocates that all property is vested in the community and work is organised for the benefit of all.

Culture: The total of inherited ideas, beliefs, values and knowledge that are commonly shared by a particular community or people.

De facto: Something which exists in fact, whether by right or not.

Democracy: A political system where most or all of the population take part in running the country usually by voting for people to represent them.

Exile: A person who is banished or expelled from his country and seeks refuge in another country.

Genocide: A deliberate killing of a race of people.

Guerrillas: Unofficial armed forces, with political motives, which resists the authority of a country usually by attacking its police and army.

Independence: Freedom for a country from occupation and exploitation by another nation. Being able to make political decision. Most decisions affecting Tibet are made by the Chinese.

Indoctrinate: To teach or instruct with a particular idea, doctrine or opinion.

Liberate: When a country is liberated it is free from enemy occupation.

Massacre: The mass killing of people.

Non-Governmental Organisation: An organisation that is involved in an international role and is free from government influence in its work.

Reactionary: A person who opposes change or tries to return to a former political system.

Reforms: Changes, hopefully for the better.

Refugees: People who have to leave an area or country to escape religious or political persecution or a disaster.

Resistance Group: A secret organisation which opposes authority in a conquered country and fights for freedom.

United Nations: An international organisation of independent states, formed in 1945 to promote international peace and cooperation.

FURTHER READING

My Land My People, Memoirs of the Dalai Lama (Potala Corp. New York, 1993)
Avedon, J: In Exile from the Land of Snows (Wisdom Publications, London, 1985)
Craig, M: Tears of Blood (Harper Collins 1992)
Gibb, C: The Dalai Lama (Exley Publications, 1990)
Perkins, J: Tibet in Exile (Cassell, 1990)

The Tibet Foundation

The Tibet Foundation is a registered charity founded in 1985. The Foundation works towards creating greater awareness of all aspects of Tibetan culture and helping the Tibetan people. Its patron is His Holiness The Dalai Lama.

The Tibet Foundation is run mainly by volunteers and is funded solely by donations.

The Foundation aims to do the following:

* To promote His Holiness the Dalai Lama's message of peace and humanity.

* To preserve and further the understanding of Tibetan Buddhism and culture.

* To support and facilitate better education of Tibetan children.

* To relieve the poverty of the Tibetan people in exile and in Tibet.

Director of the Tibet Foundation:
Phuntsog Wangyal
Administrator: Karma Hardy

For further information and membership details please contact:
THE TIBET FOUNDATION
10 Bloomsbury Way
London WC1A 2SH
Tel: 0171 404 2889
Fax: 1071 404 2366

PICTURE ACKNOWLEDGEMENTS

The Author and the Publishers would like to thank the following for use of their photographs and artwork:
Robin Bath: 4, Robert Beer: 2, 3 & 5, By Permission of The British Library: 9, Camera Press:11, Central Tibetan Administration: 12, Clive Arrowsmith & The Office of Tibet: 4, Tsering Tashi & E.D.R.C. TCV: 7, Magnum Photos Ltd & Marilyne Silverstone: 14 & 15, Ilia Tolstoy & The National Geographic: 10, Tsering Tashi & The Office of the Dalai Lama: Cover, 42 & 45, Popperfoto: 13, Tibet Images: 13, A K J Kemp & Tibet House, USA: Front Endpapers, John F Avedon & Alfred A Knopf Inc: Back Endpapers.
Every effort has been made to reach copyright holders. The Publishers would be glad to hear from anyone whose rights they have unknowingly infringed.

Tibet Offices Worldwide

The Office of Tibet
Tibet House
1 Culworth Street
London NW8 7AF
Tel: 0171 722 5378

The Office of Tibet
241 East, 32nd Street
New York, NY 10016
USA
Tel: 001212 807 0563

Getza Tibet Secours
46 Rue Llancourt
75014 Paris, France
Tel: 00331 433355582

Deutsche Tibethilfe E.V.
Wrangel Strasse 19
200 Hamburg 20
Germany
Tel: 0049 40 420 23 33

The Tibet Bureau
Rue de l'Ancien Porte
1201 Geneva
Switzerland
Tel: 0041 22 738 7940

Dept. of Information & International Relations
Central Tibetan Administration
Gangchen Kyishong
Dharamsala, 176215
India
Tel: 009118 92 22510

The Office of Tibet
Gadhen Khangsar
P O Box # 310
Lazimpat, Kathmandu
Nepal
Tel: 00977 1 419240

The Office of Tibet
Hayama Building
No 5(5F)
5-11-30 Shinjuku-ku
Tokyo - 160, Japan
Tel: 00813 33534094

Index

Amdo Province 6, 10, 12
Andru-tsang, Gonpo Tashi 12
Atisha (Indian scholar) 8

Bon religion 7-8
British connections with Tibet 9
Buddhism 31
      in Tibet 7, 8, 23
      reincarnation beliefs 35
Buxa Duar (refugee camp) 14, 31
Bylakuppe Settlement 15, 20

Carpet making 26-27,
China
      anti-Chinese demonstrations 22,
      38-39, 46
      invasion of Tibet 4, 11, 12
      occupation of Tibet 6, 12-13, 21,
      29, 46-47
      Peace Treaty with Tibet 8
      Population Transfer Programme
      5, 36-37, 44-45, 47
      Simla Convention 9
      suppresses Tibetan Uprising 4,
      12-13, 46-47
Chogden, Thupten 31
Chopak, Tenzin 43
Chou En-Lai 11
CIA 12

Dalai Lama
      early history 8
      tutors to 43
Dalai Lama, the Fifth 8
Dalai Lama, the Thirteenth 9-10
Dalai Lama, His Holiness the
Fourteenth (Tenzin Gyatso)
      at Namgyal Monastery 31
      at Tibet Support Workshop 36-37
      author's meeting with 46
      awarded Nobel Peace Prize 5, 45
      escape and exile (1959) 13-14
      Five Point Peace Plan 44-45
      Ling Rinpoche 43
      on Tibet's Independence 36-37,
      44-46
      Tibet Day speech (1994) 47
Dalhousie refugee camp 31
Deforestation of Tibet 5, 37, 47
Deng Xiaopeng 44
Dharamsala 14-15, 36-38
      Handicrafts Centre 26-27
      Refugee Reception Centre 16-19,
      40
Dharma Kings 7-8
Dolma Ling Nunnery 38-39

Dolma, Tashi 40-41
Dorje, Ngawang 24-25
Drepung Monastery 8, 11, 15, 31

Education see schooling

Fire Puja Ritual 31

Ganden Monastery 13, 15, 31
Gedhun Choekyi Nyima 34-35

Indian policy on Tibet 36

Jokhang temple (Lhasa) 7, 11, 29, 38

Kalachakra Teachings 31
Kanting Rebellion 12
Karnataka 15
Kham Province 6, 12, 16
Khampa's Movement 12
Khangsar, Mr 21, 23
Kumbum Monastery 10

Langdarma 8
Lhamo Lhatso (Tibetan lake) 10
Lhasa 6-7, 9-13
      anti-Chinese demonstrations 22, 38-39
      EC Delegation visit (1993) 16
Ling Rinpoche 42-43
Lithang Monastery 12
Losar (Tibetan New Year) 25

McLeod Ganj 16, 24, 26-27, 41
Mao Tse Tung 11
Milarepa (poet) 8
Mimang Tsongdu (People's Movement) 12
Missamari (refugee camp) 14-15, 31
Monasteries 29
      destruction of 13, 29, 38
      re-established in exile 15, 31
Mongol Empire 8
Mundgod Settlement 15
Mussoorie 14, 17, 24

Namgyal Monastery 31
Nehru, Jawaharlal 11, 14
Nepalese Border Police 16, 18
Ngawang (Tibetan nun) 39
Nobel Peace Prize 5, 45
Nomads of Tibet 6
Norbulingka Institute 29
Norbulingka Palace 11, 13

Nuclear weapons/waste 5, 37, 47

Padmasambhava 7-8
Paljor, Mr 18-19
Potala Palace 8, 11, 13
Panchen Lama 34-35

Ralpachen, King 8
Rating Monastery 11

Saka Dawa (religious festival) 31
Strasbourg Proposal 44
Sakya Monastery 8, 15
Sambhota, Thonmi 7
Samye Monastery 7
Sangmo (Tibetan nun) 38
Santarakshita (Indian scholar) 7
Schooling 17, 20-21
      personal accounts 18-19,
      22-25, 40-41
Sera Monastery 10-11, 15, 31
Simla Convention (1913-14) 9
Sonam (pupil at TCV) 22-23
Songsten Gampo, King 7
SOS Kinderdorf International 21

Takla, Mrs 20
Tashi 18-19, 40-41
Tashilhumpo Monastery 35
Tempa (Thangka painter) 29
Thangka painting 28-29
Thonden, Mrs 26-27
Tibet Foundation 48
Tibetan Children's Village 17, 20-21
      40-41, 43
      personal accounts 22-25
Tibetan Homes Foundation 20
Tibetan language 7, 17, 20-21
Tibetan National Uprising 4, 12-13, 47
Tibetan Nuns Project 38-39
Tibetan Parliament 14-15
Trisong Detsen, King 7
Tsering, Dawa 26

United Nations 11, 44, 46

Wangmo, Tenzin 24-25

Yarlung Dynasty 7
Younghusband Expedition 9
Yulgyal, Mr 16-17, 40

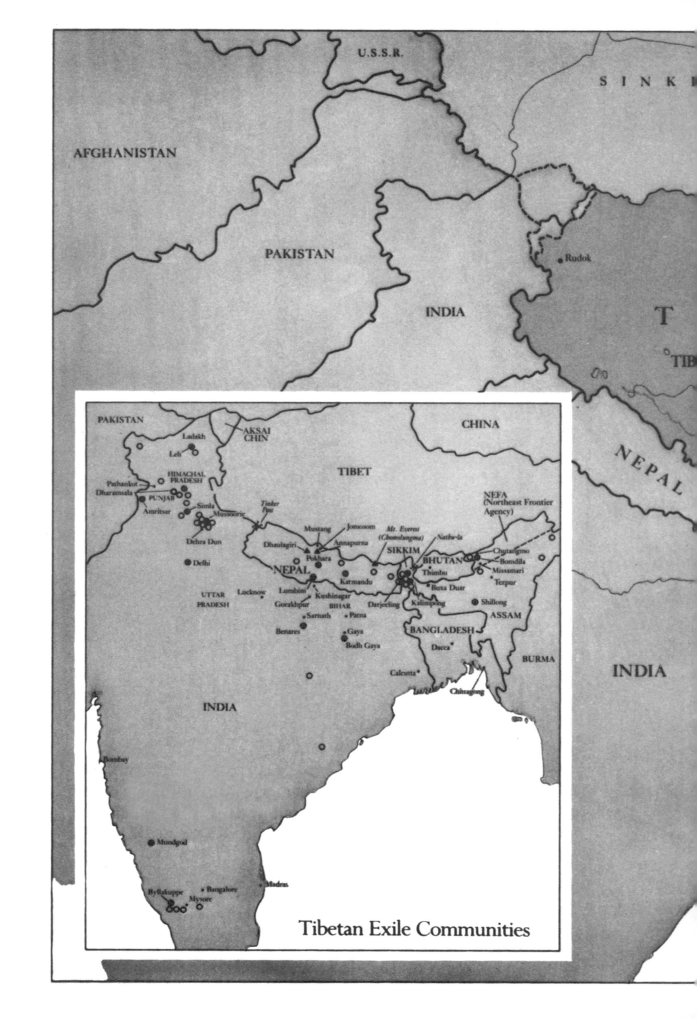

Tibetan Exile Communities